NARRATIVE SOCIAL WORK

Theory and application

Clive Baldwin

First published in Great Britain in 2013 by

The Policy Press
University of Bristol
Fourth Floor
Beacon House
Queen's Road
Bristol BS8 1QU
UK
t: +44 (0)117 331 4054
f: +44 (0)117 331 4093
tpp-info@bristol.ac.uk
www.policypress.co.uk

North America office:
The Policy Press
c/o The University of Chicago Press
1427 East 60th Street
Chicago, IL 60637, USA
t: +1 773 702 7700
f: +1 773-702-9756
sales@press.uchicago.edu
www.press.uchicago.edu

© The Policy Press 2013

British Library Cataloguing in Publication Data
A catalogue record for this book is available from the British Library.

Library of Congress Cataloging-in-Publication Data
A catalog record for this book has been requested.

ISBN 978 1 84742 825 7 paperback
ISBN 978 1 84742 826 4 hardcover

Cover design by Qube Design Associates, Bristol
Front cover: image kindly supplied by istock.com
Printed and bound in Great Britain by TJ International, Padstow
The Policy Press uses environmentally responsible print partners

To Patty and Sarah

Contents

Acknowledgements

As with all my academic writing, this book is the result of many a discussion with colleagues and friends who deserve more credit than a simple note in the acknowledgements. Their consistent and persistent patience, critical friendship and good humour have helped enormously, especially at difficult times.

I would like also to thank Karen Bowler, commissioning editor at The Policy Press, for not giving up on me after I missed deadline after deadline.

To my research assistants here at St Thomas, Carolyn Hill and Brittany Stairs, I owe much in terms of their assistance with Chapters 2 and 5 respectively. Their excellent research and notes helped me enormously. Much of the work on the chapter on meta-narratives of disability (Chapter 8) was undertaken initially by Mary-Dan Johnston and revised and extended by myself, and so the chapter appears as co-authored. Thanks also to Lauren Eagle for her final proofreading.

My especial thanks to Brandi Estey-Burtt who has far exceeded what I could have hoped for in a research assistant. Asked to produce an initial draft piece on mental health and narrative she produced an excellent text that required so little revision that it is only fair that it appear under her name alone (Chapter 7). My contribution to this chapter was more in guidance than writing. Similarly, her work on the chapter on narrative theory was of such a quality that it deserves co-authorship. It must also be noted that there is evidence of her hand throughout the book, with her careful editing, proofing and checking of references. I cannot thank her enough.

And, of course, to Patty, for bearing with me through the ups and downs of writing this, accepting the missed weekends and keeping our beloved border collie, Jagger, happily occupied while I wrote.

About the authors

Clive Baldwin is Canada Research Chair in narrative studies and director of the Centre for Interdisciplinary Research on Narrative at St Thomas University in Fredericton, New Brunswick, Canada. He has extensive experience in narrative research in the social sciences, particularly on allegations of child abuse and ethical issues in dementia. He has published on narrative as it pertains to child abuse, legal cases, ethics, personhood and citizenship, dementia and social policy. As Canada Research Chair he is engaged in research on institutional narratives, narrative literacy in professional education and narrative ethics.

Brandi Estey-Burtt has a Bachelor of Arts in English from St Thomas University and a Master of Arts in English from McMaster University, Hamilton, Ontario. She co-authored a chapter on narrative care for the forthcoming *Oxford textbook of old age psychiatry* and has been involved with the publication of a number of community projects.

Mary-Dan Johnston completed her Bachelor of Arts at St Thomas University and is pursuing a Master's degree at the University of Oxford, UK, as a Rhodes Scholar.

Part I
Narrative

Introduction

It is common now to talk of the narrative turn – the use of narrative concepts and methods – in a wide array of disciplines. Seemingly we find narrative under every stone and in every nook and cranny – narrative ethics, philosophy, theology, biology, history, anthropology, gender studies, sociology, psychology, psychiatry, medicine, rhetoric, management and leadership, and even the 'hard sciences' of mathematics, chemistry and physics. One cannot but find narrative wherever one wanders.

In social work, however – a profession that is, I think, so obviously narrative in nature – the literature on narrative is surprisingly limited. In their review of the narrative and social work literature, Riessman and Quinney (2005) found that for the largest part the literature concerned itself with narrative as a method, followed by narrative and social work education and then by autobiographical accounts. With regard to the use of narrative concepts and methods in social work research, Riessman and Quinney were disappointed by their limited use and by the variable quality of the narrative research they found. It is worth noting, however, that one exemplar that Riessman and Quinney cite explores storytelling at team meetings and addresses how cases are made through storytelling (White, 2002). This process of constructing cases through narrative has also been explored by Hall (1997), Urek (2005) and myself (Baldwin, 2005). Both Hall and Urek use narrative as a means of understanding social work per se, rather than simply an adjunct to its primary practices. This is in contrast to other authors who use narrative in a more limited fashion. Wells (2010) and Poindexter (2002), for example, use narrative simply to analyse the accounts of service users as a means of understanding those service users; Roscoe (2009) and Roscoe et al (2011) articulate narrative as a therapeutic intervention; and Gorman (1993), embraces both of these approaches; all fail to understand the fundamental narrative nature of social work. While narrative can be useful in analysis and as therapy, I believe that social work in its working up of cases, assessments, care plans, reviews and their presentation to supervisors, panels and courts is, essentially, a narrative activity. Coming closer to this view are authors such as Pithouse (1987) and Pithouse and Atkinson (1988), who analyse conversations in a social work office in terms of narrative construction, and Hall et al (2006), who explore the day-to-day language practices employed by social workers. The strengths of this form of discourse analysis lie in its focus on micro-interactions and structures in talk, analysing these from a variety of angles. A narrative approach, however, even if seen, as it is by some, as a sub-field of discourse analysis, offers something unique in its concentration on the structures that shape *stories* and *storytelling practices*, as well as being able to explore the work performed by stories within and between discourses. So while the kind of narrative analysis in which I engage here may seem to rub up against the field of discourse studies, my interest is wider and draws from literary analysis (using concepts such as genre, plot and characterisation), philosophical undertakings such as rhetorical construction, social structures and identity formation as they emerge in and through narrative, and sociological concerns with the work that narratives are called on to do in the wider world.

It is, perhaps, Parton and O'Byrne (2000) who come closest to this view of narrative and its place in social work in their discussion of what they term 'constructive social work'. In many ways this book shares their underlying assumptions and commitments to a constructivist stance, but while their text focuses on social work practice, I have attempted to provide a wider overview of how narrative shapes social work through being interwoven with social work's values, through its understanding of the individual and the individual's relationship to society, through policy development and analysis, in its ethics and, finally, through its understandings of, and applicability to, three key areas of social work practice: child protection, mental health and disability.

This approach may appear as rather different from the more traditional approaches to the use of narrative theory, and indeed it is. The rationale for adopting this approach is that as a method, perspective, process and product narrative asks new questions of, and casts new light on, not only how social work is done (akin to the works on narrative and medicine such as Hunter, 1991, and Engel et al, 2008) but also on the narrative environments in which social work is practised. In other words, this approach allows us to develop insights into social work that other, more traditional approaches, do not. By providing a language that addresses both theory and practice, that helps us understand different levels of experience and social work practice and by encouraging, if not demanding, reflexivity, narrative can provide an integrated framework for understanding fields as complex as social work. As Czarniawska (1999, p 16) says, 'narrative knowledge is an attractive candidate for bridging the gap between theory and practice. A narrative is able to produce generalizations and deep insights without claiming universal status.' My purpose in writing this book is to demonstrate the narrative nature of social work and, in so doing, promote a more critical appreciation of how social work constructs narratives about service users, about the context in which social work is done, and about social work itself. With this in mind, some preliminary remarks about the importance of narrative are in order.

For some authors, such as Barthes (1977), there is no escaping narrative:

> The narratives of the world are numberless. Narrative is first and foremost a prodigious variety of genres, themselves distributed amongst different substances – as though any material were fit to receive man's stories. Able to be carried by articulated language, spoken or written, fixed or moving images, gestures, and the ordered mixture of all these substances; narrative is present in myth, legend, fable, tale, novella, epic, history, tragedy, drama, comedy, mime, painting ... stained glass windows, cinema, comics, news item, conversation. Moreover, under this almost infinite diversity of forms, narrative is present in every age, in every place, in every society; it begins with the very history

of mankind and there nowhere is nor has been a people without narrative. All classes, all human groups, have their narratives.... Caring nothing for the division between good and bad literature, narrative is international, transhistorical, transcultural: it is simply there, like life itself. (Barthes, 1977, p 79)

Given the ubiquity of narrative, it is understandable that a narrative approach is hailed as a comprehensive way of understanding the world and ourselves. From being the subject of study and understanding, narrative has become the lens through which we study and understand, whether the subject for study and understanding is our Selves, others or the world about us.

Narratives thus operate within complex stages, associations and spheres of influence. Put another way, we can say that they simultaneously implicate different levels of experience and knowledge, each overlapping and affecting the others. These levels range from personal attitudes and emotions to our connections with our families and friends to our geographical locations and chosen communities to more general societal pressures (see Figure 1), or even any other level deemed significant to a person's situation. Usually, the stories told by our family and friends are most familiar and understandable, offering frames and schemes with which to judge input by other spheres such as community and society.

Figure 1

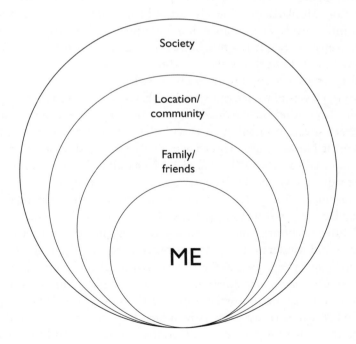

This intricate relationship can be illustrated by the following example:

The elated Girl Scout went home,

her mother proud of her for having sold all of her boxes of cookies,

those inescapable icons of capitalism,

its methods and assumptions hardwiring our children to value the power of selling in almost their every activity,

methods and assumptions championed by some and resisted by others.

Adapted from Landon (2008)

The scenario progressively moves from describing the emotional state of a sole Girl Scout to depicting the activity in which she was engaged – selling cookies – and her mother's reaction, before demonstrating that activity's links to wider social developments, in this case the ideological influence of capitalism on children. In each consecutive statement, the narrative expands from the level of the Girl Scout to broader social and cultural themes. However, as we identify the levels of narrative involved, we also weigh the successive statements against the former, measuring their validity against personal frameworks of knowledge and interpretation. Similarly, outer levels can influence how we understand and tell stories in inner levels. For instance, if a widespread social attitude argues that I should conceive of myself as a free human being with great productive capacity, I will view how I do both my work and my daily activities differently than if I were told I was a serf bound to my noble's will.

The varying levels of narrative remind us that any story we tell is always linked to a multitude of other ones. Any given story has a number of dimensions that it implicates at a given moment, such as with the Girl Scout example. In particular there are what Nelson calls 'master narratives' (what I call meta-narratives) that 'serve as summaries of socially shared understandings', often consist of 'stock plots and readily recognizable character types' and act as 'repositories of common norms' (Nelson, 2001, p 6). Each of the levels, outside of the individual, indicated earlier may have its own master narrative or narrative within which experience is shaped. Stories about 'what our family is/does' may promote the telling of some stories and hinder others – a feature seen recurrently in the family feuds depicted in soap operas such as *EastEnders*; stories about communities equally so – witness the master narratives around crossing picket lines among mining communities during the industrial unrest in the UK of the 1980s; and societal stories of what it means, say, to be British, that find their way into public policy debates or the master narratives in orthodox economic thinking of the need for development and growth. Attention to master narratives can provide insight into the values, norms and practices of a particular group, whether that group be religious, scientific, political – or social workers. We discuss master/meta- narratives in detail in Chapter 8.

The constant presence of narrative in all levels of experience is summarised by Czarniawska (2004) under the rubrics of enacted narrative as a basic form of social life, narrative as a mode of knowing and narrative as a mode of communication – in other words, as addressing ontology, epistemology and interaction. What I term the 'ontological stance', a stance that sees narrative as constitutive of the world, is reflected in writers such as Bruner (1987a, 2006), Schechtman (1996) and Ricoeur (1991), who see narrative as fundamental to being human in that we live and understand our lives in narrative fashion. But narrative is not only a way in which we understand ourselves in the world but a way of knowing, an epistemological standpoint, one which is explored by Lyotard (1984) and later Bruner (1987b) as standing in contrast to a scientific way of knowing, and by Spence (1982) and Polkinghorne (1988) as a way of knowing and a form of truth in the human sciences. Further, narrative is seen by some as fundamental to human communication and interaction (Fisher, 1984, 1985; Bruner, 1990). This way of understanding narrative – as ontology, epistemology and communication – coupled with the notion of narrative constituting different levels of experience, forms what I term the 'strong programme' of narrative thought.

The weaker version of the narrative turn holds to the view that while narrative is useful as a means of understanding individuals and the world, it does not act in a way so as to constitute those individuals and that world. The difference can be illustrated as follows, if I were to tell you a story in which, say, I rescued another person at great risk to myself. The weaker position on narrative would see this as recounting events in which I acted heroically, while the stronger position would see this narrative as performing the task of constructing myself as a hero. Or, as we shall see in Chapter 4, narrative can be seen as an adjunct to ethical reasoning in that eliciting narratives from those involved can provide rich data on which to base ethical decision-making, or narrative can be used as a means of ethical reasoning in and of itself, in which the ethical thing to do emerges from the story itself.

In locating this book within the strong narrative programme I am hoping that it will also function as an argument for that position. While there are undoubtedly difficulties associated with this position – and I will return to these later – it is one that I find fundamentally convincing. In what follows I will explore how the strong position on narrative can provide insights for the theory and practice of social work.

This strong position is, however, not always simple to understand or appreciate. When I teach my students about narrative it is relatively easy to engage them in the idea of narrative, in the weaker sense, for who does not enjoy stories and who does not have a story to tell? It is harder, at times, to help them understand the strong position, as it is less intuitively attractive and more conceptually abstract. So the question becomes, what is the relevance of the strong position on narrative to their chosen profession? It is a fair question as most of my students wish to become practising social workers rather than academics.

First, social work as a profession seeks to understand the individual in her or his social, cultural and political contexts as the baseline from which to promote social change, individual empowerment and well-being and to resolve problems in human relationships. Earlier it was indicated that narrative operates at all these levels and that a narrative approach helps us understand the theory and practice of social work. In what follows, I argue, in Chapter 2, that if we understand ourselves through narrative, then understanding the stories that individuals tell about themselves is an important way of understanding how individuals perceive themselves. If we live within a narrative environment, or web of interlocution, as Taylor (1989) phrases it, then understanding the stories circulating around individuals is important in understanding how they see others and the world. It follows, then, that if we can learn about the stories people tell, we are better placed to intervene in those narratives. If we know, for instance, that an individual feels vulnerable in certain situations, then we might wish to avoid placing her/himself in those situations until such time when we might help them address their vulnerability. If we know the types of stories that are permissible in a family and the ones that are not, then we can reflect on the best way to intervene (or whether to intervene at all). If we know the stories of different cultures, then we can act and speak appropriately in our interactions with others. And if we understand the political stories behind the situations with which we are faced, we can more effectively assess those situations and plan accordingly.

Second, if narrative is a means to understanding others, then it is also a means to understanding ourselves. Self-understanding, self-reflection and the use of Self are all core competences for social work practice, with the social work relationship and the 'self' acting as the medium through which to facilitate change (see, for example, Ramsay, 2003; Heydt and Sherman, 2005; Mandell, 2007; Reupert, 2007). Understanding who we are is, in essence, understanding the stories of which we are part (see, for example, MacIntyre, 1984, and Taylor, 1989). As social workers we are part not only of our personal stories and personal narrative environment but also part of professional narratives and the social work narrative environment. Social work as a profession has certain core narratives that influence the practice of social work and the organisations in which social workers are employed also have their own narratives – for example, many voluntary sector agencies have stories or creation myths about their founding (Schwabenland, 2006). Understanding our particular narrative environment as well as its possibilities and limitations is part and parcel of understanding ourselves in that environment and exploring the convergences and tensions between our own personal narratives and those of the organisation for which we work.

A third reason why I think narrative is important in social work is that it opens the door to examining the work that goes into creating narratives. Stories, for all their apparent naturalness, are constructions – stories have an author (or authors) who are seeking to appeal to readers. Stories do not just happen, they are made.

Events are selected for inclusion, arranged in a particular order according to the purpose of the text, given meaning or causal relationships, organised into patterns or made to stand independently and recounted in particular language – processes that I shall explore in Chapter 6. The exact configuration of these processes is a choice made by the author, with the intended readership in mind. Narrative is thus a lens through which to understand social work as authorship, authorship that restores agency and intent to social workers in their day-to-day practice.

Fourth, thinking about the wider narratives that operate in society helps to understand how social workers locate their practice in terms of how they see society. In the 1960s and 1970s there were a number of influential texts that attempted to develop an overtly Marxist understanding of social work (see, for example, the series published by Macmillan in 'Critical texts in social work and the welfare state'). While Marxism as an explanatory narrative has faded, other such narratives continue to have a significant impact on social work (for example, see Mullaly's 2007 discussion of various social theory narratives) and understanding the meta-narratives – widely circulated narratives with powerful social force in explaining events and ideas – through which social workers perceive the world, helps us understand their choice of social work theories and methods. Such meta-narratives are not always overtly political – they also operate on the level of discourse: the medical model of disability and the social perspective model of mental distress are equally meta-narratives as these frame our understandings of the phenomena with which we are dealing.

Stories also help us understand groups. Groups often have core stories to which members are expected to adhere, and knowing these stories helps us understand the internal dynamics of the group and the group's relations and interactions with other groups. Understanding the core stories of groups can help us delineate group boundaries, understand motivations and loyalties, promote group cohesion, keep discipline and justify actions. For a while I worked as a community development worker in a rural area. In one village there was a long-running dispute about the future of the village hall and whether it should be relocated. The competing stories at play were essential for understanding the various perspectives on the issue. On the one hand, there were those who wanted the village hall to remain where it was, linking it with its history, its centrality to the village centre and proximity to the war memorial and the service of its long-standing trustees. On the other, there were those who wanted to relocate the hall, focusing on a narrative of being fit for purpose in a changing environment. For these villagers the old hall was inaccessible due to its limited parking, its location away from the main road and it being no longer central to the village now that the village had expanded to include new housing estates. These competing stories were themselves interwoven with other stories about what it meant to be a villager and who had the right to a voice in the matter. Thus the debate was not simply about the village hall per se but about how different stakeholders framed the issues, partly based on their village identity.

Further, understanding the dynamics of narrative – the strategies and rhetoric of what stories are, or can be, told and how they can be told – can give us new insights into the operations of power. The denial of a narrative voice, whether coercively through force, or through more subtle operations of power such as the setting of agenda (see Lukes, 1974), can be seen as a violation of human rights, as I will argue in Chapter 1, and the development of narrative capital – a stock of stories and the authority to tell them – is fundamental to the pursuit of social justice.

It can be seen from this that the scope of this book is broad, but even so there are major areas of narrative that lie outwith its purview. First, this is not a book about method: it is not concerned with using narrative as a social work tool to institute and promote change in individuals, groups or society. Different narrative-based methods with individuals have been developed – reminiscence, narrative therapy, life story work – each having its own benefits, and there are good resources already existing on such interventions (see, for examples of these, Schweitzer and Bruce, 2008; White and Epston, 1990; Shah and Argent, 2006). The idea of narrative as a qualitative research method in social work has also been well established (Wells, 2011). Similarly, narrative work with groups is addressed partly within the literature of narrative therapy (see the resources on the Dulwich Centre website, www.dulwichcentre.com.au/collective-narrative-practice.html), partly in work on narrative and organisational change (Dunford and Jones, 2000) and partly in the literature on narrative and social change (Solinger et al, 2008). While these are important aspects of narrative in social work practice my primary concern here is of using narrative to analyse the theory and practice of social work, the narrative environment within which social work operates, the narratives told about social work from different perspectives and the insights that a narrative lens can reveal about social work practice in general.

The second major exclusion from this book is that of the role of literature in promoting social work values and ethics. In the field of medicine there is an ever-growing body of work on how literature can help clinicians develop empathy, understanding and ethical sensitivity, and there is little doubt that the same would hold for literature and social workers, although the literature is less well developed (but for good examples, see England, 1986, and Turner, 1991). While I will make reference to literary works on occasion, such references will be primarily for the purposes of illustrating my argument rather than for promoting the reading of literary works for enhancing social work practice.

Finally, media representations of, and stories about, social work are not discussed here, although these stories are very much part of the narrative environment within which social work operates, particularly as such stories tend to focus on social work failure as these stories better fit criteria of newsworthiness than the often complex and long-term nature of much social work intervention (see Galilee, 2006). However, such stories are often parasitical on, and offer little in the way of understanding, the day-to-day practice of social work.

Even with these limitations, the area to be covered is very broad and it is, I feel, incumbent on me to provide at least some guidance as to the landscape through which I wish to take the reader.

As indicated earlier, the whole of this book is really an expansion of my argument that the strong position on narrative is an important and useful way of understanding the social work enterprise. Part I, consisting of this Introduction and Chapter 1, focuses on issues in narrative theory, drawing on two main approaches. The first is fairly traditional narrative theory using concepts such as plot, character, point of view, genre and so on. Here the reader will be introduced to all the concepts needed to start to understand social work through a narrative lens. The second approach is taken from Plummer's sociology of stories (Plummer, 1994) and addresses the work that narratives do in the world. Here we see how narratives interact with other narratives, how narrators accept, promote, assimilate, recuperate, maintain, negate, challenge, undermine and silence alternative narratives and narrators.

Part II, consisting of Chapters 2 through 5, explores in detail the links between social work and narrative. In Chapter 2 I argue that certain aspects of narrative such as voice, dialogue, contingency and uniqueness are directly relevant to the realisation of social work values. In Chapter 3 I explore issues of narrative and the Self, indicating how we can understand our Selves and others through narrative. Arguing against an essentialist view of the self, I move toward the notion of the Self as rhizomatic, a term taken from the work of Deleuze and Guattari (1987), or, in other words, a Self characterised by complexity, multiplicity, non-linearity and decentred-ness. This notion of Self, I argue, is one in which self-authorship is central and one which respects the commitment of social work to the uniqueness of individuals, enabling or empowering them to take control of their own lives in the pursuit of their own goals.

In Chapter 4 I turn to ethics. Social work is, fundamentally, a moral endeavour. It sets itself the task of helping individuals to change and to change society in accordance with its value commitments and underlying principles. It is not so much that there is an ethical aspect to social work, but as an evaluative activity social work itself is an ethical enterprise. As such I argue that narrative ethics can accommodate or incorporate diversity in a way that normative ethical frameworks cannot, and that it restores ethical accountability to the heart of social work practice.

Finally, moving on from the individual, in Chapter 5 I turn to the relationship between narrative and social policy. In some ways, this is the least well-developed area of the narrative turn. While there has been some interesting, and, to my mind, persuasive work done by Roe and others (Roe, 1994; Fischer, 2003: Hampton, 2011), narrative seems to have had less of an influence on mainstream social policy than it has perhaps had elsewhere. Nevertheless, through an analysis of policy examples it is possible to explore the relevance of narrative to social policy.

In Part III I use three fields of social work activity – child protection, mental health and disability – to illustrate in more detail the application of narrative in understanding social work. Chapter 6 explores the notions of character, plot, authorship, readership and rhetoric as they manifested themselves in a case of alleged child abuse. In exploring these narrative features I will attempt to illustrate the role of rhetoric in social work narratives. Chapter 7 turns to mental health, and in particular, how the Self is conceived and constituted in mental health discourse. While a narrative approach is gaining some ground in mental health, there is still a strong tendency to view mental illness as, at best, disrupting the Self, and at worst, resulting in the loss of Self. In exploring the Self during times of mental distress we can argue that narrative provides the means to preserve the Self and that we might look to alternative ways of understanding and intervention that promote narrativity. Finally, Chapter 8 focuses on disability and meta-narratives – those over-arching stories that frame our understandings of others and the world. As regards disability we see, over time, changing meta-narratives, from the religious or moral model in which disability was seen as divine retribution through the deficit-focused medical model to the social perspective and, more recently, citizenship models.

In the concluding chapter I discuss some of the advantages and limitations of the narrative approach, attempting to deal with some of the criticisms that have been raised about the ubiquity of narrative, before inviting the reader to return to the text to apply the narrative approach that I have advocated therein.

1

Introduction to narrative theory

Authored with Brandi Estey-Burtt

If we are to understand social work as a narrative activity it is, from the outset, important to understand something of narrative theory. Narrative theory is riddled with arcane terminology – terms such as fabula and sujet, diegesis, mimesis, hermeneutic and proairetic codes and so on – that can make it difficult to approach at first. It is not my purpose here to delve into great depth but rather to provide a basic understanding of some of the main features of narrative and ways of exploring narrative that have relevance to understanding social work. The first section of this chapter identifies major features of narrative easily familiar to most people on a day-to-day basis, such as plot, characterisation, genre and so on. The second section introduces three approaches to narrative – formalism, a sociology of stories and framing and canonicality – which may help in developing informed interpretations of stories in the field of social work.

While in this book I focus primarily on analysing documents, the process of narrativisation begins much earlier in the talk between social workers and service users, in social work offices, and in meetings made up of people from different organisations and the assessments, case notes and reports and so on can be seen as end products of this process. Just as Atkinson (1995) has demonstrated how medical personnel reason, discuss, create and judge the evidence before them in the process of diagnosing, treating and assessing progress, so too do social workers 'work up' their assessments, interventions and progress reports through talk (see, for example, Pithouse and Atkinson, 1988). Although I intend here to concentrate on the written narratives of social work, many of the features discussed below are as applicable to talk, to conversation, as they are to text.

Seven features of narrative

Plot

For many readers, plot represents the exciting twists and turns that a story takes as it creatively describes a sequence of events. Scholes and Kellogg (2006, p 207) point to this understanding when they identify plot as 'the dynamic, sequential element in narrative literature.' They refer to plot in terms of action alone, but Forster (1927) tends to view characters as an essential aspect of plot as well. However, Abbott (2002) adds somewhat more nuance to the definition, noting that plot has become somewhat of a catch-all term equivalent to the idea of story itself. He thus carefully distinguishes it from story as 'how the story is conveyed', otherwise called narrative discourse in narrative theory (2002, p 13). We might also call this emplotment, or the artful arrangement of the story.

This arrangement can take many forms. According to Aristotle, a beginning, middle and end are necessary, as is some sense of unity and/or internal coherence. For Forster (1927), causality assumes great importance, leading the reader and demanding that they intelligently engage with the story and how it is represented. On the other hand, Propp (1968), in working with Russian folktales, argued that there are a limited number of plot functions peculiar to those folk stories. Some of them are readily familiar – for example, what may be called the quest undertaken by the hero but complicated by a villain is a stock type in many different media of storytelling. Plot is thus remarkably versatile in the way it can be ordered, the style it can take and the characters that can be part of it. It is usually assumed to take place in some sort of time frame, but the sequencing of this is also unrestricted. Hence, we can have flashbacks and flashforwards, or a purely linear chronological succession of events.

Regardless of what elements are variously attributed to it, plot stands out as one of the most crucial aspects of narrative. Novels, movies, plays, television shows, and so on are easily noticeable as forms that deliberately and carefully use plot to convey both information and the goings-on in a story. However, emplotment is a universal activity embedded in everyday life as people regularly use emplotment in daily conversations to describe their activities and relationships. This practice also extends into other common forms such as news articles, official case reports, and most certainly social work presentations (see Hall, 1997). In these instances, it structures how knowledge and actions are organised and presented. This is both a very deliberate and a very precise activity, as the order and lay-out of facts and information has a critical effect on the reader. We shall see this at work in Chapter 6 when I examine in detail competing narratives of child protection. For now, however, it is enough to note that emplotment can influence the reader to think that a given outline of a story is the only plausible or logical one, discouraging other attempts at plotting the same narrative differently (see Hall et al, 1997; Hyden, 1997), and can, therefore, be used to produce specific meanings in regards to a particular social work case, constructing incidents and behaviours a certain way rather than another.

Characterisation

In the writing on literature there is a debate as to the relative merits and importance of plot-driven and character-driven narratives. Plot-driven narratives are those that then tend to focus on action; character-driven narratives on the individual or individuals who are acting. Of course, good stories have elements of both – even thrills and spills action movies have to have appropriate characterisation – plot and character go together. As Henry James put it, 'What is character but the determination of incident? What is incident but the illustration of character? What is a picture or a novel that is not of character?' (James, 1884, p 6).

The importance of characterisation is that without believable characters the narrative will fall flat. To be believable the characters must be recognisable, demonstrate convincing motivations and be authentic, that is, act according to character. This focus on moral character is what Strong (1979), in writing about the medical professions, termed 'character work'. In the sociology of medicine, Strong (1979) talks about character work, that is, how medical personnel construct parents in terms of moral character – for example, whether they are 'good' parents. While such work might be done in private, and medical staff might not be overt in their condemnation of parents, their inquiries provided material from which 'indictments could always be made' (Strong, 1979, p 154), potentially identifying or giving grounds for suspecting, or attribution of responsibility to, the parents. This form of character work is, perhaps, more overt in social work, especially in cases of suspected child abuse. In discussing social work and the construction of unsuitable mothers, Urek writes: 'In characterisation ... social workers make available different attributes of characters of their clients. Through different narrative strategies they let us know about "what sort of persons we are dealing with"' (2005, p 453). Indeed, in some cases such as those of alleged Munchausen syndrome by proxy, character work is inherent within the operationalisation of the concept and investigation of suspected cases (see Baldwin, 2004).

While characterisation is part and parcel of social work, this should not be taken to imply that characters so formed have to be 'round' in Forster's sense – that is, built around complex and multifaceted features – or undergo development that may surprise the reader (see Forster, 1927). It is enough that they are appropriate to the plot. Indeed, characters that are 'flat', that is, uncomplicated, static, two-dimensional, may serve the plot far better than more developed, three-dimensional ones (see Clay, 2000). Two-dimensional, unsurprising characterisation might incline the reader to believe that such individuals are incapable of change and thus will always act in the way they have acted. We see this in some social work assessments where a parent might be characterised as uncooperative, non-compliant, hostile, in denial, and so on, and thus the best interests of the child are served by removal from the birth family. A more rounded characterisation, one indicating development and change, might undermine such a care plan. Alternatively, in arguing for the preservation of the family, a social worker might round out the character of the parents to support a plan for intervention and reunification. Characterisation can thus act as a rhetorical device to persuade the reader as to the appropriateness of the response to the situation (see Pithouse, 1987; Urek, 2005).

Characterisation may also be implicit, that is, one learns about the character of an individual from one's thoughts, actions and words, from passing references, assumptions and interactions with others. In social work texts implicit characterisation is often used in regard to other professionals and predominantly portrays professionals as benevolent and benign (see Ingleby, 1985). There is often the assumption that other professionals are competent, objective, trustworthy and reliable – subtly indicated by taking their statements uncritically when supportive of the case to be made; and even when there is disagreement the focus is on the evidence, interpretation and argument rather than the character of the individual. In this, there is often a distinct a–symmetry of characterisation in social work texts (see Baldwin, 2005). Thus, when thinking about social work reports it is important to bear in mind how the subjects of those reports are being characterised and positioned with respect to one another. The issue of characterisation is explored at greater length in Chapter 6 in relation to allegations of child abuse and the construction of the 'dangerous mother'.

Genre

The term 'genre' refers to the categorisation of texts by style, form or content. In literature and film there are many genres and sub-genres, ranging from romantic to horror, epic to science fiction, and combinations of these, such as the comedy-gangster movie *Pulp fiction* or the musical horror production of *The rocky horror picture show*. Beyond these more conventional genres, there are numerous genres of texts related to the necessities of work, home and everyday life. Academic writing could be considered one such genre, as could internal work reports, case studies, medical charts, and so on. They all have boundaries related to what may be discussed and how it is to be presented.

The importance of genre lies in a number of functions. First, a recognisable genre allows the reader to locate the piece within a framework that is familiar, one that is indicative of what can be reasonably expected. Genres help manage the expectations of the reader by being 'relatively stable types of utterances' that help the reader understand the expressions, relations, meaning and boundaries contained within (Bakhtin, 1986, p 60), and in so doing provide us with a framework within which to understand the text, anticipate its development and frame our response. So, for instance, in the romantic drama *Love story* one can expect the inclusion of ups and downs in the relationship between Ryan O'Neal and Ali MacGraw and for certain emotions to be aroused. Similarly, one can expect an absence of zombies, cowboys and intergalactic battles. At the same time, however, it means that genres 'delimit the scope of interpretation' (Pyrhönen, 2007, p 114), meaning that when a reader implicitly acknowledges a genre as a framework of interpretation for a text, they simultaneously cut off other possible interpretations of that text. Reading *Huckleberry Finn* only as an entertaining story for children limits one from seeing its powerful social commentary.

Further, the requirement of genre might influence the content and style of the text. In terms of content, for example, a tragedy usually necessitates someone in the story dying. In regards to style, a classical detective mystery such as those written by Agatha Christie involves a lighter tone and less blood and guts than the thriller-type mysteries written by James Patterson. This notion of genre-shaping the pragmatic design of the text certainly extends to social work: 'Discourse regulations [established by genre – CB] determine what *can* and *cannot* be discussed as well as what *might* and *must* be discussed' (Paré, 1998, p 112). Risk assessments, social reports, case conferences, care plans, even contact notes and referrals can be seen as constituting particular genres, requiring the inclusion of specific information, the use of specific language and the acceptance of the values, norms, customs and habits of the workplace. So, Paré's (1998) discussion of predisposition reports demonstrates the impact of that genre on what constitutes admissible and inadmissible evidence and the potential consequences of stepping outside the discourse boundaries. Similarly, in their study of therapists' interactions with their clients, Berkenkotter and Ravotas (1997) demonstrate how the clients' narratives are transformed into therapeutic concepts and categories, which then form the defining framework for the relationship.

Finally, learning to write in the particular genre(s) of the profession can be seen as a means of socialising individuals into the particular goals, activities and identities of the profession; thus, maintaining adherence to genre can be interpreted as adherence to the values, norms and ideologies embedded within professional practice. In Paré's words, 'Such a genre set shapes a unity of approach and conceptualization within the community of practice; it shapes in large part the development of the individual's thinking with others about the client through the mediating structures of the genre set' (Paré, 2000, p 156).

In this way, genre is a powerful indicator of the stylistic and thematic features of a text, reader expectations and possibilities of interpretation. Importantly, genres also point to 'ways of seeing and interpreting particular aspects of the world, strategies for conceptualizing reality' (Pyrhönen, 2007, p 121). It is therefore necessary to be aware of the way they produce and shape expectations and attitudes regarding individual texts.

Point of view

Point of view refers to the perspective or position of the narrator from which the story is told. Customarily, there are certain possibilities for this perspective with the first person and third person being most common, although these two exhibit numerous variations as to how each are employed or mixed. In first person point of view, narration proceeds from an 'I', a person, either a character or a narrator, who describes events from their personal understanding. In terms of grammar, the third person comments on all characters as 'he', 'she', 'it' or 'they'. An external narrator relates information about characters or events. In the *Harry Potter* series, for example, the narrator usually takes the third person form, limited to the knowledge of story events found out by Harry's character. A number of scholars in narrative theory dislike these distinctions, preferring Genette's (1972) more technical understanding of hetero- vs homo-diegetic narrators, but the conception of point of view here will serve us for the present moment.

There can be several narrators in a story, each presenting a very different perspective than another. Furthermore, their point of view may be expressed in a multitude of formats: orally or written in diaries, letters, reports and so on. In *The Guernsey literary and potato peel pie society* (Shaffer and Barrows, 2009), the narrative is entirely composed of letters. A number of people are engaged in writing the letters, thus offering many perspectives, most of them from the first person point of view. News items and social work reports, however, try to maintain a third person viewpoint in the attempt to portray objectivity, even if there is a person reporting. They seek to be detached from the events depicted, although they cannot entirely excise certain value or belief judgements from their narration.

A major consideration of point of view stems from its function as an articulation of a narrator. This in turn leads into questions of reliability. How trustworthy and reliable is the information and material presented by this particular person speaking? In other words, can I believe what the narrator is telling me? This has been a potent literary question for a number of years now, but its implications extend far beyond traditional storytelling to encompass daily narrative activities. If a person tells me they just saw a unicorn walk down the street, I am going to doubt both the existence of the unicorn and the overall reliability of the person. I do not simply take the person's veracity for granted.

This activity may be applied to all sorts of stories, ranging from smaller stories such as sibling disputes (one of them ate the cookie no matter what they both claim) to larger political narratives (most people tend not to take the election policy platforms of political parties at face value, instead suspecting other interests at play in them) and even to courtroom proceedings (all parties involved put a certain spin on the evidence presented). Thus, paying attention to what a narrator is saying and their motives in saying it is a crucial pursuit inextricably linked with deciding who is doing the telling in the first place. Thus, in the case discussed in Chapter 6 we can ask – even if we cannot be certain of the answer – why the social worker fabricated or misreported events, and reasonably make inferences from these fabrications as to the reliability of the narrator and her motives, both of which could have significantly affected the course of the proceedings had they been taken into account by the judge.

Rhetoric

Rhetoric, despite its modern-day negative reputation replete with connotations of manipulation, duplicity, emptiness and lack of ethics, is, more technically speaking, simply the art of suasion, either persuasion to a particular view or action or dissuasion, away from a particular view or action. Moreover, for Aristotle, rhetoric, properly used, performs an important function in determining what is or can be known, and gives epistemic grounds for being able to rely on what is said. It is this positive function of rhetoric that is of interest to us in our exploration of narrative and social work for, if we can enhance our skills in determining the reliable from the unreliable, the trustworthy from the untrustworthy, and the robustness of evidence and testimony of others, then we are in a better position to undertake our work, work that often has serious implications for others. In Chapter 5 I explore some of the rhetorical features of the National Dementia Strategy (NDS) and in Chapter 6 how an understanding of rhetoric might have prompted a more critical approach to the case and have prevented a miscarriage of justice. At this point, however, I simply want to lay out some of the key principles of rhetoric.

For Aristotle (nd) there are three divisions of rhetoric: the deliberative or political, in which the speaker seeks to persuade the audience toward or away from a particular course of action; the epideictic or ceremonial, in which the speaker is concerned with the praise and blame of their subject; and the forensic, in which the speaker seeks to establish the justice or injustice of some action or other. Each of these is concerned with a different aspect of time as its primary focus. Deliberative rhetoric focuses on the future, what is to be done either for the good, in the case of arguing for a particular course of action, or in order to avoid harm, in the case of arguing for the rejection of a course of action. Epideictic rhetoric concerns itself primarily with the present, as praise and blame rest on the state of things existing at the time. Forensic rhetoric focuses on the past, being concerned with establishing what happened as the basis for judgement.

In practice the three divisions of rhetoric may merge, the boundaries becoming blurred. In child protection proceedings, for example, the concern might be initially to determine what happened (forensic) as a basis of establishing who is responsible for the harm caused (epideictic) and determining the appropriate course of action (deliberative). The three-fold division, however, is important as it provides a tool with which to identify the different types of argument and their relative strengths so as to allow us to apportion appropriate weight and attention to each and to explore how each might affect our understanding and acceptance of the others. So, for example, while it might be the case that we like to think that forensic rhetoric takes precedence over the other two divisions – the establishment of what happened as the basis for our allocation of responsibility and our choice of course of action – in practice, the here and now can affect our interpretation of the past. For example, in one case of alleged child abuse, the father of the index child refused to leave his wife, accused of harming a previous child by another relationship and potentially harming the index child, until the allegations were proven. This refusal, based on the primacy of forensic rhetoric, was viewed by the social services and courts as indicative of collusion or denial (epideictic), thus casting doubt on the father's testimony as to what happened (forensic), and thus influenced the formulation of the care plan for adoption (deliberative) prior to any allegation being tested in court. In other words, for the father the appropriate process was to establish what happened, allocate responsibility and then determine on a course of action (forensic, epideictic, deliberative). In the argument of the social services the three were not clearly demarcated, with each playing into the other.

Within the three divisions of rhetoric, Aristotle argues that there are three forms of rhetoric: ethos, pathos and logos. Ethos is an appeal to the honesty, trustworthiness, credibility and character of the speaker – in social work, this might be made manifest through seeking professional evaluation or an expert witness for court proceedings where the position and reputation of the person is important in their opinion being sought. In narrative terms we can speak of reliable and unreliable narrators (see Booth, 1961; a narrator is unreliable if s/he misreports, misinterprets or mis-evaluates or, alternatively, under-reports, interprets or evaluates, factors which speak to the honesty, credibility, trustworthiness and character of the narrator). Pathos is an appeal made to the emotions, values or interests of the audience – for example, to the 'best interests' of the service user, to the paramountcy of the welfare of the child or the protection of the vulnerable. Logos is the appeal to logic, reason and argumentation, that is, the power of facts and evidence arranged in such a way that each step follows from the previous one. The persuasiveness of the logos rests on either example or syllogism. In the case of argument from example, the speaker rests their case on inductive logic – for example, this person has a history of this particular behaviour and is thus more likely to exhibit this behaviour in future. This is logic based on probabilities and the conclusion is not inherent in the argument and is thus not absolutely certain. In the case of syllogistic reasoning the logic is deductive and the conclusion must follow from the premises – for example, if a child's welfare is paramount in child protection proceedings and these are child protection proceedings, then in these proceedings the child's welfare is paramount. We shall see both aspects of logic at work in Chapter 6.

In addition to these classical divisions and forms of logic two other elements of rhetoric need to be introduced as related to our overall theme of narrative in social work. First, there is the level of explicit detail – what appears as persuasive on first reading might be less so when further details are introduced, or, of course, what appears unconvincing at first may be more persuasive once we know more (see Bartlett and Wilson, 1982). Further detail pertaining to a situation might provide an alternative explanation or indicate mitigating circumstances that make the original story less convincing. Second, there is the notion of narrative coherence, where a coherent story is more likely to be persuasive even if untrue and an incoherent one unpersuasive even if true (see Bennett and Feldman, 1981). Coherence itself is the result of a number of choices on the part of the author: for example, the omission of discrepant or disruptive material, the smoothing of the story elements (Spence, 1986) and the structuring of the plot, elements we shall see in Chapter 6.

Social workers engage in rhetoric when they seek to persuade others. Writing reports, undertaking evaluations, preparing care plans, applying for resources or funding are all attempts to persuade others to one or other course of action (and thus dissuade from other courses of action). Assigning or mitigating responsibility or simply attempting to describe events leading up to the present situation in a credible manner are all exercises in rhetoric. For example, a social worker writes a report for the courts outlining a case and in so doing puts forward a care plan involving adoption of a child outwith the birth family rather than a plan for reunification. The purpose of the report is to present this course of action as the appropriate response to the circumstances and to have the courts agree with the recommendation. The rhetorical strength of the report will determine whether or not the care plan is accepted or rejected.

Authorship

The idea of the author has been one of the most significant in storytelling, although it has come under much fire in recent decades in literary and narrative theory. Nevertheless, the concept of the author as producer of a text or story is one of the most immediately identifiable to the majority of people who consume texts. Strictly speaking, the idea of authorship indicates a person (or persons) who is the originator of a particular narrative. Furthermore, as Phelan (2006, p 209) argues, this person or author produces a narrative 'in order to affect readers in particular ways.' The author has a story in mind and proceeds to use various narrative devices such as emplotment, characterisation, point of view, time, rhetoric and so on to bring life to the narrative. In the case of written works, this process usually culminates in a material text that may be disseminated to other people to read.

As with most things in life, however, the idea of authorship is not always so simple or clearly demarcated. For instance, the author's relationship with the reader must be taken into account, not just the process of textual design and production. Who is the author writing for? How does this expectation of prospective audience manipulate or affect the author's process of shaping the text? If I write to persuade my readers to share my opinion on a topic or issue, my text will be very different than that written solely for entertainment purposes. Similarly, the affect produced in the readers will be quite diverse in each scenario. Authorship therefore does not exist independently of those for whom the text is constructed.

There is also another important distinction to be made about authorship. Just because so-and-so writes a book does not mean that they reveal all their heart and soul in that very book. Often, an author chooses how they want to be understood by the reader as the author of the text or the reader infers a sense of the author from their reading – this is what is known as the implied author (not the narrator of the story). Recognising that authorship is not so straightforward as commonly seems enables one to realise that the process of meaning-making in storytelling is never one-sided or innocent. Like the narrator and their own particular point of view, the implied author may not be entirely reliable or may construct a sense of her/himself in order to persuade the reader to form certain opinions about the text. This is certainly something to bear in mind as we are inundated with texts and stories on a regular basis, often from authors with conflicting opinions and ideologies.

Bakhtin (1986) further identifies two important corollaries of the voices articulated by the author: polyphony and heteroglossia. Polyphony involves multivoicedness, or the expression of multiple voices, Selves and perspectives that are not necessarily the author's own but are all given equal status by the author. Heteroglossia refers to the social meanings embedded in the use of all language, informed by our involvement in multiple social contexts simultaneously and consequently imbued with ideology and the stylistic residue of various discourses.

Authorship is also linked with rhetoric. Social workers, in writing reports for court, making the case for services or applying for funding, are writing for a particular audience at a particular time. Furthermore, for the narrative to be accepted it needs to appear more credible and persuasive than the alternatives presented on. While social work texts are often written in the third person we can make inferences about the implied author and her/his reliability, expertise, motivations and values, thus allowing us further insight into the production of this text at this time, insight that might significantly affect our understanding and interpretation of that text.

Readership

If the author is ostensibly the originator of a work, then the reader is the person who consumes that work. They come to a given text prompted by a variety of factors, including a text's genre, content, recommendations and so on, and judge the text in accordance with expectations shaped by those factors. The reader also necessarily brings with them their own attitudes, experiences and modes of understanding, all of which affect their interaction with each new text. This interaction prompts the reader to make meaning out of what is going on, a process otherwise known as interpretation.

As with the implied author, there can also be an implied reader, and it is once again important to be aware of the difference as it affects one's ability to read and to make sense of a story. The implied reader is the author or narrator's conception of the ideal reader of this particular text. As actual readership can vary across historical time periods, 'race', class, gender, and so on, the text is produced with a certain reader in mind. For example, the implied reader of Jane Austen's early 19th-century novels is much different than a female university student who might pick them up in the 21st century for a course.

Readers thus abound when narratives are presented, and all will have dissimilar, possibly contradictory interpretations. They can also read for very different patterns of meaning: what they think the author's intended meanings of a story are, what they posit are the author's unconscious meanings unintentionally revealed in the text and how they would like to adapt the story to new issues or other media (Abbott, 2002). For example, in the case described in Chapter 6 it is possible, from the documentation, to identify places where the judge read into the evidence his own interpretations of the parents' characters and behaviours, interpretations not necessarily and certainly not conclusively or unambiguously supported by the evidence but which make far more sense when we take into account that the judgment was not only prepared for the parties to the proceedings but also anticipating a reading of the case by the Court of Appeal, a Court that might read the case differently and thus undermine the judge's own narrative.

By interpreting the parents' characters and behaviours in one way rather than another, the possibility of alternative readings by new readers may be curtailed.

Readers are therefore a critical component of the author/text/reader relationship. Authors can try to persuade readers to choose particular interpretations, or readers can understand that all authors and texts have background motivations as an indispensable part of their makeup. Everyone comes to the text with radically different expectations and knowledge and this makes reading an extremely unpredictable activity, although authors attempt to discern and map possible reader reactions and incorporate this information into their design (see Urek, 2005).

Having discussed our seven aspects of narrative we now turn to three approaches to narrative: formalism, the sociology of stories, framing and canonicality to round off our discussion of narrative theory.

Three approaches to narrative

Formalism

Formalism refers to a type of literary analysis that focuses on the structure or form of any given text rather than on the author's background or social or historical influences. As a literary movement, formalism is often associated with a number of scholars in Russia working prior to Stalin taking power. They emphasised the 'functional role of literary devices' (Leitch et al, 2001, p 1060) as a means of analysis and evaluation. In other words, they looked at aspects of form that make a particular type of writing distinct.

Propp (1968), although not necessarily labelled a formalist, noted that the specific combination of events in a text is marked by what he called recurring functions. These functions may be mixed and re-ordered in any number of ways while still adhering to the basic purpose of the function. So, for instance, we often see the unrepentant evil villain, the compassionate helper or the conquering hero in stories of all types. Propp primarily worked with Russian folktales, but his identification of reappearing plot and character functions has been useful in other areas of study such as media and film scholarship, and we can see such functions in social work texts where the roles or helper, protector, supporter, colleague, villain and so on are reproduced in almost stereotypical fashion. Urek (2005) describes well the portrayal of Ana as an unsuitable mother and the contrastive characterisation of the foster mother as 'a real saint' and other professionals as protectors of the child.

With formalism, then, we can ask certain questions such as how a text works and what narrative strategies are at play in regards to the plot that help produce the overall story. These questions are valuable in examining other types of texts to learn how internal mechanisms combine to create the noticeable features of those texts. For example, social work reports may be considered a genre abiding by pre-set expectations of form and content. We can analyse these reports formally by explicating the narrative devices and strategies they use to produce the finished text. Moreover, such plot and character functions as outlined by Propp make their way into these types of texts as well, potentially shaping how a reader views a person, as seen in Urek's (2005) case study of Ana who is constructed and presented as an unsuitable mother with resistance being shown to alternative readings of the situation. It is thus possible to do a character/role analysis of the figures in a social work text and question how they are being represented.

Sociology of stories

A story is thus made up of complex parts, each with many different ways of being combined, presented, interpreted and analysed. However, the telling of a story with all of these elements involves a number of processes. This certainly includes the ideas of authorship and readership, as described earlier, but it also points to external societal processes influencing which stories may be told in the first place and even how they can be told. Plummer (1994) identifies five elements of stories which are useful in outlining the wider frameworks of power in which storytelling is always inv   ... the nature of stories: (2) the making of stories; (3) the consuming c   n the wider world.

The natur   ces, giving agency and empow   dominating others (Plummer, 1   d in this way, such as in the exam   other professionals as benevole   e marginalised and excluded, w   nd more credibility' (1994, p 29

The sec   oduction of stories, asking wha   stories possible and how could   he consumption of stories, Pl   of storytelling – the reading o   vith the text. It also initiates q   place and how their social situ

Plumm   people and groups use diverse narrative strategies to tell their stories. These strategies could range from the internal mechanisms at work in the stories themselves, mechanisms such as language and the aspects which we have been discussing earlier – plot, character, time, genre, point of view, and so on – to social concepts employed to structure a story – Plummer cites the idea of women's stories being more non-linear than those of men (1994, pp 29-30) – to ways of using the body to tell stories. These strategies are incredibly varied, but they all aid in the creation of certain impressions in the reader or listener.

The last element is that of stories in the wider world, and it outlines the connections between stories and the social worlds in which they are produced. This means examining what social conditions and frameworks of power are in place allowing certain stories to be told, others to be silenced, and still others to be told in very specific terms. It also ties in to the fact that stories have various levels of significance in different historical and social moments. Although the national story of British imperialism held great cultural and historical power in the 18th and 19th centuries, that story has since been re-evaluated in the context of stories from groups and peoples which it disenfranchised and disempowered.

Plummer's five elements take us beyond analysis of how a text fits together to an understanding of how stories undeniably shape and are shaped by social, historical and personal processes. Stories move in and out of power relations as they seek to persuade, entertain, inform and educate their readers, and it is necessary to realise they are always influenced by external motivations.

In Urek's work (2005) we can see each of these elements at work as Ana was constructed as an unsuitable mother, certain voices being given space to be heard and not others (notably Ana's), lost opportunities for alternative narratives, societal narratives of acceptable patterns of relationships and appropriate maternal behaviour; and in my own work on contested allegations of Munchausen syndrome by proxy I have illustrated the strategies and rhetorics involved in the interplay of competing narratives (see Baldwin, 2004).

Framing and canonicality

Framing and canonicality are interrelated concepts founded on the notion that people organise current knowledge into categories and use cognitive procedures that help them make sense of the world. Stemming from the work of Goffman (1974), the concept of framing has been adopted and adapted within narrative studies as a means of understanding how readers make sense of, make meaning from and evaluate new narratives. Frames, sometimes also referred to as schemas, are ways in which one's previous knowledge of stories act to shape contact with new stories, how new stories are received by individuals who either incorporate them into their existing pool of stories or reject them as incompatible with, or disruptive of, that pool of stories. Bruner (1990, p 56) observes that, 'Framing provides a means of "constructing" a world, of characterising its flow, of segmenting events within that world.' Framing is thus remarkably similar to schematising, which provides a cognitive means of organising and classifying knowledge. This activity has consequences for a number of cognitive processes: 'A schema is a category in the mind which contains information about a particular subject.... [They] help us assign meaning to incoming information.... Schemas also help us select the information we will pay attention to ... [they] also allow us to draw inferences, based on our schematic hypotheses, about what is likely to happen in the future and what has happened in the past' (Moore, 1989, pp 279-80). Schemas or frames thus provide interpretive models for how we interact with different stories that come our way. They scour the new narrative for associations with prior stored knowledge and then allow us to construct meaning based on any parallels that emerge. This process is therefore limited to the experiential knowledge we have on hand, possibly curtailing different approaches to processing and interpreting fresh information or even distorting those processes and interpretations (see, Sherwin,

1994). This has ramifications for reading stories that do not fit the mould of our existing frames and schemas, an idea associated with canonicality.

Canonicality acts as a sort of measuring stick for stories, gauging how a certain story performs when compared to what is generally understood to be the template for a canonical narrative in a particular area, and narrative smoothing occurs when there is an 'attempt to bring the clinical assessment into conformity with some kind of public standard or stereotype' (Spence, 1986, p 212). Bruner (1990, p 47) links canonicality with a focus on 'the expectable and/or the usual in the human condition. It endows these with legitimacy and authority.' This relates to what Berger (2011, p 279) refers to as 'tacit knowledge and unconscious assumptions and inferences.' She remarks, 'Because the tacit knowledge we have acquired through experience is at work automatically and always, it can remain uncontested.' Canonicality then represents a shared set of norms based on mutual knowledge and experience that is legitimated by the status of common sense but which is often not consciously examined or explicated.

Anything deviating or being exceptional to this idea of canonicality will be exposed to a meaning-making process seeking to recover links to canonicality (Bruner, 1990, p 49), with a possible judgement or evaluation of whether it is a 'good' story or a 'bad' one stemming from how well it fits with the canonical template. As Bex (2009, p 1) points out, a good story should be well-structured (understandable) and plausible, with a 'plausible story correctly describ[ing] a general pattern of states and events one expects to come across in the world.' Those stories that do not fit with canonical expectations and recognisable patterns are deemed 'bad' and subject to negative evaluation. So, for instance, if a narrative by someone with mental health troubles does not exhibit linearity, coherence or organisation – features thought to characterise canonical narratives in general – their story could be treated as symptomatic of their 'illness' and overwritten by the medical narrative of their need for forced treatment. The stakes are thus very high when it comes to understanding stories in terms of canonicality, with those not proper to it possibly being ignored, silenced or co-opted by canonical stories.

Canonicality can thus act as a rhetorical strategy – the more a particular narrative can be made to appear to conform to an already accepted stock of stories, the more likely it is to be accepted into that stock. We shall see this strategy being employed in Chapter 6.

Further reflections

This introduction to narrative theory will hopefully provide an orientation for discussion of narrative in future chapters and the terms, concepts and methods of analysis they employ. Understanding these features of narrative is the basis for understanding how stories act in the practice of social work. For example, it is possible to see child protection reports as framed within the genre of a romance, as defined by White (1973), in which good triumphs over evil (the child is saved from her/his abuser), with Proppian characters of hero, villain, helper and so one being filled respectively by social workers and the courts, the 'perpetrator' and other professionals. While this example is a rather crude application of genre theory to social work, reading social work case notes and reports one is left very much with the impression that underlying the ostensible neutrality of professional language is a narrative genre that frames what is and is not permitted. Paré (1998), for example, demonstrates how the genre of predisposition reports (reports written by social workers for courts prior to sentencing an adolescent) reflected and reinforced the knowledge and beliefs of the social workers and what they expected of the adolescent. Similarly, we shall see in Chapter 6 how plot, characterisation and rhetoric served to bolster the credibility of the narrative that the mother under examination posed a danger to her daughter, despite evidentiary and logical holes in the argument.

This discussion of the features of narrative, however, is by no means comprehensive, and I will introduce other terms as I progress. But for now, it will serve as a starting point and useful primer to general understandings of how stories work and the strategies they employ.

Part II
Narrative and social work

2

Narrative, human rights and social justice

Up to this point we have been concerned with laying out the fundamentals of narrative as a lens through which to understand social work as an activity. Here we explore the relationship between narrative and social work more directly, first by examining the areas of social work values before moving on to discuss narrative in relation to the Self, ethics and social policy.

As of the time of writing (January 2012) the British Association of Social Workers (BASW) is revising its *Code of ethics* in social work. Given the similarity of the draft (available via BASW's website at www.basw.co.uk/) to the ethics in social work *Statement of ethical principles* of the International Federation of Social Workers (IFSW) and International Association of Schools of Social Work (IASSW), it is unlikely that any significant changes or divergences will emerge prior to its adoption.

The ethics of social work (BASW, 2011) is, in all essentials if not in terminology, identical to that of the IFSW (2004) in defining and outlining the essential values of social work. Each of these values – human rights and dignity, social justice and professional integrity – is underpinned by five principles, although I am primarily concerned with the first two of these here (see Table 1).

Table 1: BASW values and principles

Value	Underpinning principles
Human rights	Upholding and promoting human dignity and well-being
	Respecting the right to self-determination
	Promoting the right to participation
	Treating each person as a whole
	Identifying and developing strengths
Social justice	Challenging discrimination
	Recognising diversity
	Distributing resources
	Challenging unjust policies and practices
	Working in solidarity

Source: BASW (2011)

In what follows I will take each of these and discuss aspects of narrative that are particularly relevant in understanding the relationship between social work values and narrative. In so doing I am not suggesting that there is a neat and tidy, one-to-one relationship between each of the underpinning principles and a feature of narrative theory, but that, more broadly speaking, taking into account narrative can help realise the values on which social work is based. This chapter, therefore, consists of two substantive sections – one on each of the values – to which we now turn.

Narrative and human rights

In Chapter 1 I discussed the concepts of authorship and narrative agency. Authorship, I suggested, is the ability and opportunity to construct our own story our own way(s), in our own words, on our own terms and for our own purposes. In this way it is fundamental to the process of becoming, in the Deleuzo-Guattarian sense – and to understanding, maintaining and expressing ourselves individually and in relation to others. Related to this is the notion of narrative agency, that is, the idea that we are actors in the stories that we author rather than marionettes controlled by the stories of others. In essence, these are two elements to 'narrative voice' – having a voice to construct a story and having a voice within the story so constructed.

The United Nations (UN) Universal Declaration of Human Rights (UDHR) (UN General Assembly, 1948) states that everyone has the right to freedom of thought, conscience and belief (Article 18) and the right to freedom of opinion and expression (Article 19). These two fundamental rights can be expressed in narrative terms as the right to a voice, whether an inner voice through which we construct and understand ourselves and our world or an outer voice through which we present ourselves to, and interact with, that world. Of course, these voices are not discrete, and as we have seen in the previous chapter, polyphony (many voices) rather than monophony (one voice) shapes our narratives of Self and the world. But the point stands, I think, that whatever this voice or these voices, individuals have the right to create and express stories about themselves and their world without undue interference from others or the state.

Further, the UDHR makes provision not only that everyone has the right to a voice but also that everyone has the right to have their voice heard at least in publicly sanctioned institutions such as in the right to a fair hearing (Article 10) and the right to participate in government, the will of the people being the authority on which government rests (Article 21).

Lest you are by now thinking that I am stretching the argument rather too far in attempting to make the links between human rights and narrative voice, I would ask you consider the following.

Between 1954 and 1962 France and Algeria were at war. During this time the French police and military systematically employed torture in an attempt to maintain control of the colony. One case of such torture, involving Djamila

Boupacha, received great attention through an article written by Simone de Beauvoir for *Le Monde*. In discussing this case, and the issue of torture more generally, Slaughter (2007) argues that torture 'directly attacks the victim's ability to narrate (or even think) a coherent self-image' (p 11), 'targets the subject's ability to narrate her experience by fracturing integrating linguistic structures through "the question" and confession' (pp 11-12). Furthermore, 'torture replaces the tortured's voice with a voice supplied by the torturer', a process that also seeks to employ the voice of the tortured against herself. This attack on narrativity was recognised, according to Slaughter, in the UN Convention against Torture and Other Cruel and Unusual Punishments, Article 15, that invests torture victims with a redefined power to narrative, 'That is, the tortured voice can legally narrate the destruction of that voice as evidence against the torturer' (Slaughter, 2007, p 12).

While this is, no doubt, an extreme instance, I suggest that the principle remains the same when we scale down the stakes and the violence – namely, that the denial of voice undermines the dignity and well-being of the silenced, excludes them from participation and prevents us from understanding the whole person and how s/he might author her/his own story. I illustrate this with a far less dramatic example, perhaps even mundane in comparison: that of dementia care and how people living with dementia might be dispossessed of their narrative in a number of ways.

A fundamental aspect of narrativity is being able to tell one's story. This narrative agency depends on:

- being able to express oneself in a form that is recognisable as a narrative, even if one's linguistic abilities are limited (see Booth and Booth, 1996; Goodley, 1996);
- having the opportunity to express oneself narratively.

To express oneself narratively requires a degree of conformity to narrative rules or habits or customs. Adherence to such rules, habits and customs might vary in degree but it becomes apparent that beyond a certain threshold, 'differences of degree effectively become differences of kind; beyond that point a sequence may begin to display so little narrativity that it can no longer be processed as a story at all' (Herman, 2002, p 100). Consider the following from Herman:

1. A bad man walked in. Then a beneficent sorcerer pulled the lever, and the bad man was instantaneously inebriated.
2. A splubba walked in. A gingy beebed the yuck, and the splubba was orped.
3. Oe splubba fibblo. Sim oe gingy beebie ca yuck, i ca splubba orpa.

The first of these is easily and straightforwardly recognisable as a narrative. The second, while unintelligible in terms of what actually happened and to whom or what, is recognisable as a narrative: first this happened, then that. The third displays zero narrativity because it 'lacks sufficient grammatical structure for recipients to infer actants and entities populating a story world' (Herman, 2002, p 102).

For those living with dementia the difficulties encountered with expressive language, loss of memory for recent events and disorientation to place and time may limit the possibility of engaging narratively with the world and with others. Utterances may appear to others as lacking in meaning due to the person's difficulty retrieving the correct word from memory or difficulty putting words in the correct sequence along with the mis-identification and difficulty retrieving the characters, events or context. If one expects a higher degree of conformity to narrative rules, habits or customs, then it is possible that one would see people living with dementia as losing narrative agency sooner rather than later.

The second element of narrative agency is having the opportunity to express oneself narratively. People living with dementia, however, find themselves narratively constrained in two ways. First, opportunities for narrative expression are limited: people living with dementia may experience a loss of control, in that decisions are made for them (and stories made about them) as they are increasingly defined as lacking capacity, and a loss of narrative opportunity because of lessened opportunity for social interaction. Second, the mental space within which narratives can be told is constrained through the mobilisation of the meta-narrative of dementia which defines the person in terms of decline, loss and fragmented cognitive functioning (and thus less able to tell a recognisable narrative) and the recuperation of expressions of agency (such as 'wandering', 'challenging behaviour', fidgeting) as symptomatic of the dementia itself (see Kitwood, 1997).

A second feature of narrativity is a sense of consistency and coherency that holds together (more or less tightly) the events, characters and context in an understandable whole. For example, Polkinghorne (1995) suggests that there should be historical continuity of characters because such continuity enables the reader to understand the characters as individuals, acting on, but not determined by, their history. By paying attention to the context and embodiment of the protagonist and to the significant others in the story a successful narrative establishes a backdrop against which to evaluate the narrative. The story emerges from this backdrop in a way that does not disrupt one's belief in or jars with the backdrop, that is, it does not appear as a disruptive episode that has no links with the past or future. Furthermore, the choices and actions of the protagonist should make sense against this backdrop and cohere with what we know of the protagonist. In other words, for a narrative to be successful, the historical continuity of backdrop, story and protagonist is maintained.

People living with dementia, however, may not display such narrative consistency or coherency. Events may be forgotten or remembered only partially or erroneously; characters may be forgotten or mis-remembered and the context of the story being told may not always be the expected one. So, a long dead character may appear alive, well and functioning in the narratives of people living with dementia because the person with the dementia has forgotten the death of that person; sons may be remembered as husbands or not recognised at all; and the story being told might not be consistent with the context or other stories previously told. In such circumstances the accounts of people living with dementia may well appear confused, contradictory, irrational or unintelligible and as such, may not be acknowledged as narratives at all.

Third, there is emplotment, the process whereby events, characters and context are positioned in relationship to one another in such a way that the story moves from one position to another. This formulation of a narrative trajectory, realisable through time, is essential to narrative and is dependent on consistency and coherency. The difficulty this poses for people living with dementia is not only that events, characters and context may become confused, but also that the forgetting of the nature of things and the loss of memory and sense of time makes it far more difficult to emplot a story. Living progressively in the present with gaps in short-term memory and little conception of the future, it is hard to envisage how people living with dementia might construct a meaningful narrative.

People with dementia thus experience a loss of narrativity. Historically this has been seen as a result of the dementia as the condition compromises the ability of the individual to formulate and articulate a narrative. While this might be the case, I wish to turn this around and suggest that it only does so because those without dementia cannot recognise non-standard narratives, that is, narratives that do not conform to the rules and norms of the cognitively able. To conform to the narrative rules and norms of the cognitively able (and indeed, all those whose narratives might fall outside of the current rules of narrative – those, say, with autism, experiencing mental distress or those with amnesia or stroke) we dispossess them and thus deny or silence their voice and in so doing assault their human rights.

While my first offering for consideration focused on how violations of human rights involve the distortion, negation, fragmenting or silencing of narrativity and voice, my second turns to the promotion of human rights through providing an environment in which that voice can be heard and stories narrated, that of the Truth and Reconciliation Commission of South Africa. Established to deal with the abuses committed under apartheid in South Africa, the Commission clearly had recourse to narrative. The Promotion of National Unity and Reconciliation Act No 34 of 1995 charged the Commission with:

> … establishing as complete a picture as possible of the causes, nature and extent of the gross violations of human rights which were committed during the period from 1 March 1960 to the cut-off date, including the antecedents, circumstances, factors and context of such violations, *as well as the perspectives of the victims and the motives and perspectives of the persons responsible for the commission of the violations*, by conducting investigations and holding hearings (www.justice.gov.za/legislation/acts/1995-034.pdf, emphases added)

and

> ... establishing and making known the fate or whereabouts of victims and by *restoring the human and civil dignity of such victims by granting them an opportunity to relate their own accounts* of the violations of which they are the victims, and by recommending reparation measures in respect of them. (www.justice.gov.za/legislation/acts/1995-034.pdf, emphases added)

The importance of having a voice and to be listened to is emphasised in volume one of the Truth and Reconciliation Commission report where the Commission states that '... its purpose in attempting to uncover the past had nothing to do with vengeance; it had to do, rather, with helping victims to become more visible citizens through the public recognition and official acknowledgement of their experiences' (TRC, 1998, p 110), and cites Thenjiwe Mintso, opening the Commission's hearing on women in Johannesburg on 29 July 1997:'[This hearing] is the beginning of *giving the voiceless a chance to speak*, giving the excluded a chance to be centred and giving the powerless an opportunity to empower themselves' (TRC, 1998, p 110; emphases added).

At this level of operation narrative served as a means of gathering information, which:

> ... in the hands of the Commission made it impossible to claim, for example, that the practice of torture by state security forces was not systematic and widespread; that only a few "rotten eggs" or "bad apples" committed gross violations of human rights; that the state was not directly or indirectly involved in "black-on-black violence"; that the chemical and biological warfare programme was only of a defensive nature; that slogans by sections of the liberation movement did not contribute to killings of "settlers" or farmers; and that the accounts of gross human rights violations in the African National Congress (ANC) camps were the consequence of state disinformation. Thus, disinformation about the past that had been accepted as truth by some members of society lost much of its credibility. (TRC, 1998, pp 111-12)

But the Commission recognised a deeper importance of narrative, that the process of 'establishing truth could not be divorced from the affirmation of the dignity of human beings' because, 'the process whereby the truth was reached was itself important because it was through this process that the essential norms of social relations between people were reflected' (p 114). In other words, 'the Commission not only helped to uncover existing facts about past abuses, but also assisted in the creation of a "narrative truth"' contributing to reconciliation 'by ensuring that the truth about the past included the validation of the individual subjective experiences of people who had previously been silenced or voiceless' (p 112) and thus 'recovering parts of the national memory that had hitherto been officially ignored' (p 113).

Thus we have one of the most significant reconciliation processes in history recognising that voice and narrative are inextricably linked with human rights and dignity and the establishment of truth.

Again, an extreme example, but the point can be seen as applicable to more mundane activities. If we return to the three elements of narrativity – narrative agency, coherence and consistency and emplotment – compromised by the onset and progression of dementia but ultimately denied by how they are understood or interpreted by those without dementia, we can see how, by reformulating these elements, we can promote narrativity and thus respect the human rights of those involved.

There are three ways of promoting narrative agency when linguistic ability is compromised. The first is to seek to narrativise other symbolic means of expression. Stories can be articulated, for example, as much through dance, movement and artistic expression as they can language – if we, as readers, are sensitive enough to the narrative features of such media, and this is, of course, a familiar and common approach in the arts. Similarly, Downs et al (2006) cite literature from Norberg and colleagues (2003) demonstrating the effectiveness of communication styles including affirmation, confirmation and communion. They also cite the growing use of sound, music, dance and movement in making contact. Observational methods such as dementia care mapping (see Brooker, 2005) encourage us to adopt an empathic stance to our understanding of a person's experience throughout the day.

Second, we look towards the joint authorship of narratives where the narrative process is shared by people living with dementia and those around them. This may take the form of co-construction of narratives (see Keady and Williams, 2005; Williams and Keady, 2005) whereby the final narrative is very deliberately and consciously a negotiated product between those people living with dementia and others or the piecing together and progression of the fragmented narratives of people living with dementia by those who support them:

> The person with moderate or moderately severe dementia may be able
> to present only fragments of a performance story. The more a nurse
> knows about narrative components or the different sections of a story,
> the more easily he or she can identify and follow up on a story fragment
> offered by a person with dementia. (Moore and Davis, 2002, p 263)

The third way to reconfigure narrative agency is to examine the contribution made by people with dementia to the narratives of others. This, in good part, is to understand the nature and role of reading in the process of narrativity. Illich (1996), in commenting on Hugh of St Victor's *Didascalion*, differentiates between monastic and scholastic reading. Scholastic reading, he says, views the text as an object to be debated (What is the author saying here?) while monastic reading was an embodied activity that viewed the text as having something to say directly to one's experience and existence (What does this text say to my life?). It is my contention that by viewing the text of another's life in this latter fashion we are opening the door to re-establishing some degree of narrative agency through the other's story, contributing in a meaningful fashion to our own life narratives.

If we turn now to reconfiguring narrative consistency and coherency, while the narratives of people living with dementia may at times appear to be fragmented, inconsistent and incoherent, this may be seen as a function of an insistence on linear consistency and coherency rather than as inherently associated with dementia. We might, for instance, choose to reconfigure consistency and coherency to accommodate a sort of patchwork of fragments, individually uncertain in meaning or narrative value, into a meaningful whole. Moore and Davis (2002) refer to this as narrative quilting. Stories are thus related, not necessarily to what immediately preceded them but to other stories that have been told by or about the person living with dementia. The narrative consistency and coherency then rests not in chronology but in the assemblages of fragments related by meaning. The accurate reading, and meaningful assembly, of such fragmented stories requires the sort of narrative competence that Montello refers to when discussing the benefits of engaging with literary narratives (Montello, 1997, p 194): 'joining one story with another, accurately to observe and make sense out of the chaos of suffering and loss.'

Our final reconfiguration centres on the notion of emplotment. I suggest that rather than insist on a narrative trajectory that is maintained over a reasonably lengthy period of time, we focus on what Bamberg calls 'small stories', stories that privilege the fleeting and fragmented as contributing to the performance of identity in everyday interactions (Bamberg, 2004). Given the 'present-ness' of people living with dementia, such a focus would seem to be highly appropriate and, from Bamberg's work with adolescents, an effective means of recognising, acknowledging and supporting the creation and maintenance of Selves through the minutiae of everyday life. What is required is the ability to skilfully read and collect such small stories over different times and places so that they may be knitted into patterns that can be used to support the personhood of the person living with dementia. Emplotment thus becomes a process of assembling, over time, small stories that are related to one another in terms of expressions and developments of the Self in the face of changing circumstances. Linear emplotment thus makes way for thematic or semiotic emplotment.

In drawing this section to a close I go one step further and suggest that there are still other ways that we, as social workers, might act to dispossess others of their narratives and thus infringe on our basic value of human rights. Take, for example, the assessment or investigative process whereby we seek to gather information about the situation and the person in order to make an assessment and form a basis for future action. In interviewing service users do we ask questions in such a way that open up space for the expression of narrative agency and the development of narrative, or do our questions fragment any emerging narrative by focusing primarily on those elements that we see as important without regard for the importance of narrative continuity between those elements? Do our narratives serve to close down alternatives or open up space for new narratives? Similarly we need to pay attention to the sort of meta-narratives we employ to interpret or explain situations or make sense of individuals' stories. Meta-narratives may contribute to narrative dispossession in two ways. First, meta-narratives might act to constrain narrativity by allowing only certain stories or types of stories to be told. For example, in the case of P, C & S (see Chapter 6) the meta-narrative of medical and social welfare professions as both benevolent and benign prevented an alternative narrative of incompetence, malevolence and lack of professionalism (all of which had evidence enough to support at least a hearing) from being developed, the alternative narrative being recuperated into the narrative of Munchausen syndrome by proxy (MSbP) as denial or smokescreen or further evidence of MSbP behaviour. Second, meta-narratives might serve to frame service user narratives in ways that support the meta-narrative but undermine that of the service user. For example, Little and Hoskins (2004) suggest that it is the meta-narrative of the *Diagnostic and statistical manual* that constructs what it means to the an anorexic girl, with the impact that such a construct has on self-concept.

In asking these sorts of questions it is clear that narrative dispossession does not have to be the result of dramatic acts of narrative negation but can be the result of our day-to-day practices and so, becoming narratively literate – that is, sensitive to the ways narratives are recognised, solicited, treated, interpreted, managed and so on – is important if we are to uphold human rights.

Narrative and social justice

I now look at the relationship between narrative and social justice. This flows naturally enough from the link between human rights and narrative, and extends our understanding of how narrative issues are inextricably intertwined with these two social work values. It is established by authors such as Ewick and Silbey (2003) and the contributors to the collected editions by Davis (2002) and Solinger, Fox and Irani (2008) that narrative plays an important role in the struggle for social justice. Citizens and service users, carers and professionals employ personal and community narratives as a strategy for raising awareness and challenging unjust practices and policies.

Here I explore the interplay between the personal, social and political embedded in every narrative. These dynamics of power play a crucial role in determining which stories are heard, acted on and celebrated, and which are kept hidden, separate from the public sphere.

In Chapter 1 I referred to Plummer's sociology of stories and the need to explore the nature of stories, that is, 'Which kinds of narratives work to empower people and which degrade, control and dominate?' As social workers, we come face to face with all of these issues in our practice. Narratives of control and domination emerge when imbalances of power are present. Such imbalances might be visible and extreme, for example, in the case of domestic violence in which someone is subject to severe degradation, control and domination at the hands of a perpetrator. Domestic violence as a form of psychological dominance creates an ever-growing power imbalance between victim and perpetrator, leaving the victim feeling dependent on the abuser. As the abusive relationship slowly chips away at the victim's self-worth, a new reality of dominance and control unfolds. The narratives of the abuser and the abused are separated by an extreme imbalance of power.

Imbalances of power may also be subtle and covert such as in the ability to define the situation in which one finds oneself. Cast (2003) argues that individuals can control the definition in three ways: by behaving in ways consistent with their identity, by influencing the behaviour of others and by resisting the identities that others, in turn, attempt to impose on them. Those with more power are more able to realise each of these. Take, for example, a social work assessment interview. The social worker is undertaking a task that is entirely consonant with his or her social work identity. Indeed, it is through tasks such as assessment interviews that the social worker's identity is made real. On the other hand, the assessment interview may be threatening to the identity of the service user who may be assessed in ways that do not resonate with their sense of identity. For example, in child protection cases the social worker may be assessing a parent to decide whether or not their parenting is good enough to allow the child to remain at home; in mental health assessments the social worker may be assessing whether or not the individual should be allowed to remain in the community or be detained as being a danger to themself or others, regardless of how the service user perceives themself. In cases such as these the identity of one party is secured by the very task itself, while the identity of the other is the subject of the task. Attempts by the service user to redefine the situation as one of intrusion into private life, the practice of oppressive forces, examples of incompetence and so on may be recuperated into the social worker's definition of the situation as hostility, denial or lack of cooperation.

The key to overturning narratives of dominance is to identify and challenge the imbalance of power. If the narrative of dominance is overt or maintained by violence, then the development of alternative stories that challenge the narrative of dominance, that is, counterstories, requires finding niches in which to tell subversive stories or exploiting tensions and fissures within those narratives. The first of these is illustrated in Mike Beckham's film *Tiny revolutions* (1981), in which a Czech professor is imprisoned for telling anti-Soviet jokes: 'Czechoslovakia is buying a navy' says one person. 'Why would Czechoslovakia need a navy, it's landlocked?' is the response. 'We have a Ministry of Justice', says the first. The second, taking Nelson's example, is illustrated by the claims of some Christian groups that women are not permitted to be church leaders, often citing 1 Timothy 2:12 as scriptural authority for their reasoning. However, in Acts 18:26 there is an example of a woman speaking publicly without any remonstration – undermining the exclusory interpretation (see Nelson, 2001).

If, on the other hand, the narrative of dominance is more subtle and less overt, one may have to undertake a degree of deconstruction of the hidden messages within that narrative. A good example of this is Mumby's (1987) analysis of narrative in the service of organisational ideology and power structures. For Mumby,

> Narratives are not generated in a socio-economic vacuum but are an expression of the material conditions that a particular mode of production generates. The process of narrative helps to reproduce these material conditions by articulating an internally coherent sense of itself and the world that it describes. In other words, narratives punctuate and sequence events in such a way to privilege a certain reading of the world. They impose an order on "reality" that belies the fact that such a reading is a largely ideological construction that privileges certain interests over others. (1987, p 126)

Taking as his example a narrative about the (white male) chief executive officer (CEO) of IBM being challenged by a female supervisor on his entrance to a security area in an IBM building – a story itself taken from Martin et al (1983) – Mumby demonstrates how the story masks sectional, corporate interests, how it reifies the positions of the male CEO and his entourage and the female security officer and how it acts as a means of illustrating and consolidating how people are expected to act within the corporation.

This process of deconstruction can take place at a number of levels. First, as in narrative therapy a social worker might help identify oppressive narratives (see White and Epston, 1990) and work with service users to construct personal counterstories. Second, one might reflect on the ideological functioning of social work narratives that often mask organisational interests, confirm professional positions (such as professionals being benevolent and benign; see Ingleby, 1985) or limit service users' actions while deploying the language of empowerment (see, for example, Brandon, 1991; Solas, 1996).

Nevertheless, narratives of empowerment often play a crucial role in the struggle for social justice. In the book *Telling stories to change the world* (2008), Solinger, Fox and Irani bring together a collection of powerful stories about ongoing struggles for social justice. From this highly diverse collection of narratives, one key theme emerges: the narratives identify obstacles (for example, to freedom or to health) and respond by giving voice to visions and dreams for a better world. As Solinger et al write in their introduction: 'The story becomes a way of remaking the world; being a storyteller in these contexts means being an activist' (2008, p 6).

In one such story, the reader is introduced to the Neighbourhood Story Project in New Orleans, a collaboration between teachers and students at a high school better known for 'shootings, fights, and 80 percent [of students] not passing the exams required for graduation' (Breunlin et al, 2008, p 75). When two dedicated creative writing teachers realised that many of the issues driving students away from formal schooling were economic, they decided to offer students a chance to make money by writing books about their neighbourhood blocks. Seven students signed on and became paid authors working with the Neighbourhood Story

Project. The students progressed from researching to conducting fieldwork to writing and editing their very own books for publication. Sharing stories about everyday life in their own blocks allowed the students/authors to introduce the outside world to areas of New Orleans often relegated to brief segments about gun violence on the evening news. After Hurricane Katrina, the stories became a source of inspiration for families and communities from these blocks as they began to rebuild their lives and houses. For those who were evacuated from the city, the stories reminded them of home. The Neighbourhood Story Project empowered students to become authors of their own community narratives, defining their neighbourhoods on their own terms while challenging the dominant narratives shown on the evening news.

In other cases, authors fight hard to be heard, often drawing on incredibly creative strategies in the process. In their work on the use of stories in citizens' resistance to authority, Ewick and Silbey (2003) recount many such stories. In one example, a middle-aged African-American woman used her knowledge of hierarchies of gender and 'race' subordination to her benefit. Unable to secure a service from a telephone company, she telephones the company president and tells his secretary that she is his housekeeper. She is put through to the president and immediately outlines her complaints about the poor service she has received from the company thus far. As Ewick and Silbey explain,

> [She] drew on her racially marked speech and her knowledge of the back doors of formal organizations to manipulate a conventional expectation that African–American women serve as domestic workers for white elites, thus circumventing her lack of power in her legitimate consumer role. (2003, p 1353)

In another example, the mother of a child with special learning needs engages the tactic of colonising space to help her son get what he needs from his high school guidance counsellor. After her son is unable to obtain a copy of his transcript for college applications, she occupies the guidance counsellor's office, refusing to leave until she is able to speak with the counsellor. Her efforts are successful, and she recounts,

> So I didn't like to have to interfere like that but I learned back in elementary school when other mothers use to do it, and I used to be the type who didn't say much and sat back, that other parents were getting what their kids needed for them.... So I had to change my way and I had to start speaking up. (Ewick and Silbey, 2003, p 1362)

Ewick and Silbey (2003) argue that the sharing of stories of resistance is an important act of resistance in and of itself, a slight re-authoring of the power hierarchy inherent in structures of institutionalised authority. In telling stories of resistance, the 'taken for granted social structure is exposed and the usual direction of constraint upended, if only for a moment' (p 1329).

While the telling of stories may act to promote social justice, the silencing or censoring of certain stories may act to hinder it. Dominant narratives, as indicated earlier, might be maintained through the silencing of alternative or oppositional narratives. In the most extreme cases, this plays out as government censorship. In the Islamic Republic of Iran, for example, government censorship touches many aspects of everyday life. Sparked by the Arab Spring movements in Egypt and across the Middle East, pro-democracy protesters rallied in Tehran in February 2011, calling for an end to the hard-line Islamic regime of President Mahmoud Ahmadinejad. Protesters were beaten by the police and dispersed using tear gas; there were reports of at least one fatality. In Iran, however, government television channels had shown a few carefully chosen images from the rally, and explained to viewers that a pro-government rally had taken place in Tehran. A story that was deemed important on the other side of the world was not available to many citizens of Iran. Such silencing, however, is not restricted to authoritarian regimes. Cases involving allegations of child protection in the UK are held in camera, thus restricting the audience from hearing the stories being told. This is ostensibly to protect the child but has also served to protect the interests of social services and the courts when publicity would have exposed potentially unprofessional or illegal behaviour or the violation of human rights. For example, in the case of P, C & S discussed in Chapter 6, the parents were threatened with contempt of court if they spoke to the press concerning the case, a case that violated the human rights of both the parents and the child whom the social services and courts were supposed to be protecting (see, for example, Baldwin, 2008a).

The notion of availability of stories moves us on to the notion of narrative capital. The notion of narrative capital is developed from Bourdieu's (1986; Bourdieu and Passeron, 1990) concept of cultural capital that refers to assets such as information, contacts and skills that, while non-economic, provide individuals with a distinct advantage compared to those lacking these assets. I suggest that narrative capital is a form of cultural capital in a number of ways. First, given that narrative is an inherently persuasive means of communication (see Fisher, 1984), the ability to tell a good story is part of linguistic capital and thus helps position storytellers according to their narrative abilities. Second, the stock of stories to which one has access is important – if one has only a few, isolated stories then these may not be sufficient to challenge the meta-narrative of a dominant group, but if one has access to many stories this may position one strongly in such a challenge. For example, if a single service user reports abuse while in residential care it is easier for this to be covered up or dealt with than if several or many service users report similar stories. The cumulative effect of stories is what forced the investigations into abuse at Haut de la Garenne children's home and eventually forced an apology out of the government of the island (see, for example, Pidd, 2012). Similarly, if one has access to a wide range of stories one is in a better position to respond flexibly and creatively to new situations. If, as I have suggested in Chapter 1, we frame our ongoing experiences in terms of stories that are familiar to us, then the more limited our stock of stories, the more limited the possible frames we have for understanding. Conversely, if we have a wide range of stories, we are more able to appreciate and promote diversity in situations that we face. Each of these aspects of narrative capital can contribute to the promotion of social justice. For example, being aware of stories of success may help motivate others – say, in community groups campaigning for change; being aware of the stories of others in similar situations may help us press for changes to policies and procedures; and being aware of stories of particular cultures may help us understand others more clearly and help us act with cultural competence. Finally, working with service users to develop their narrativity, their ability to construct and articulate their stories may result in significant change not only individually but also collectively. Freire's concept of conscientisation (1972), the raising of awareness among peasant groups, was based on helping them formulate narratives about their political situation – see the description of the process in Freire (1974) and Arnett and Arenson's (1999) discussion of Freire and narratives of liberation.

Social justice requires that we challenge oppression, whether that oppression be through exploitation, marginalisation, powerlessness, cultural imperialism or violence. Narrative and narrativity have a part to play in the promotion of social justice. Narratives can help develop collective identities and solidarity (see Polletta, 2002 and Benford, 2002) and in so doing lead to action. As Fine (2002, p 238) says: 'Stories bind individuals to each other as they recognize that they have common experiences that shape their identity and their linked futures. As a result, this perspective is both retrospective and prospective. Stories – and discourse in general – represent a processing of a shared past ... and through this creation of a shared past, coordination of action emerges.' Providing spaces for oppressed people to find a narrative voice challenges the marginalisation caused by silence, challenges the powerlessness caused by the de-legitimising strategies of meta-narratives and challenges the consciousness infiltrated by dominant, interest-led narratives (see Nelson, 2001).

Operating at the level of the individual voice or at the level of community or society narratives can force others to take note: 'In Chile, it is no longer permissible, to assert in public that the Pinochet regime did not dispatch thousands of entirely innocent people' (Ignatieff, 1996, p 113, cited in TRC, 1998, p 5).

Further reflections

In this chapter I have attempted to make apparent the links between narrative and human rights and narrative and social justice. In so doing I have adopted the strong programme of narrative outlined in the Introduction, that is, a way of viewing human rights and social justice through the lens of narrative, rather than simply looking at narratives *about* human rights and social justice. In so doing, I hope also to have further demonstrated how this approach to narrative differs from that of previous writings on narrative and social work. If my argument so far has been at least somewhat persuasive it is incumbent on me to articulate at least some ways that this narrative understanding of human rights and social justice might have an impact on the practice of social work. Further examples will become apparent in later chapters – for example, in the links between the Saying and the Said in Chapter 4 on narrative ethics, which addresses issues of narrative voice, or the advocacy for a rhizomatic understanding of disability in Chapter 8 – but here I want to mention just two.

First, that social work needs to re-establish a focus on collective action. Much, although by no means all, of social work currently focuses on the individual case. While community resources may be accessed in order to support the individual, these do not necessarily adopt a collectivist approach. For example, Home-Start provides essential support for families with young children under pressure, but local groups tend not to adopt a collective programme of action to challenge existing social structures that create those pressures in the first place. Similarly, many service users access social services as a result of poverty and while help may be available to individual service users in the form of welfare benefits advice, say, from Citizens' Advice Bureaux, there is little in the way of collective organising that we saw in the 1970s in the form of Claimant Unions (see Rose, 1973; Cannan, 1975). In so doing, social workers need to understand the relationships between individual narratives (the lived experiences of service users) and the meta-narratives of society, exploring how alternative narratives can be generated, supported and maintained through collective action.

The second impact I want to raise is that of solidarity with service users. If we accept that narrative is part and parcel of social work practice, human rights and social justice, then it is not enough simply to work with the narratives of service users and movements for social change but to become part of those stories. This involvement, this solidarity, can be expressed in two ways. First, through involvement in those social movements to which we point service users as equal partners and involvement in trades unions, community groups and party politics (see Corrigan and Leonard, 1978); second, through participatory social work that involves practitioners, local people and service users on equal terms (see Beresford and Croft, 1980; and the Social Work Action Network at www.socialworkfuture.org/) and participatory social work education (see Richardson and Beresford, 1978, and, more recently, the Social Work Education Participation Project at www.socialworkeducation.org.uk). In part this is a recapturing of the radical social work of the 1960s and 1970s (see Brake and Bailey, 1975) that was eroded and lost in the 1980s and 1990s (see Langan and Lee, 1989), but a narrative approach goes further in that it ties together social workers and service users in mutually constituting stories (see Chapter 3 on the narrative constitution of the Self and Chapter 4 on narrative ethics). In effect this is a re-storying of social work, akin to the individual re-storying advocated by proponents of narrative therapy (see, for example, Abels and Abels, 2001) that creates a narrative environment in which social work can attempt to realise its commitments to human rights and social justice.

3

The narrative Self and social work

There is a large and ever growing literature on the relationship between narrative and the Self. My purpose here is not to review the myriad theories of Self – theories that cut across disciplines such as philosophy, social sciences, psychology, literature – but to introduce a number of ways narrative has been used to understand the Self and how each of these might have something to say about social work. In the Introduction I suggested that there are stronger and weaker positions on narrative depending on whether one sees narrative as reflective of life or the world, or as constitutive of life and the world. The same, I suggest, is also relevant to how we see the relation between narrative and the Self. Accordingly, I have arranged the all too brief discussions of Self and narrative below in order of increasing narrativity: from narrative as reflecting an essential Self about which narratives may be told to a rhizomatic Self that is constituted solely in and through narrative. My starting point, however, is an assumption that narrative is in some way part and parcel of the Self.

Broadly speaking, the literature on the relationship between narrative and the Self can be seen along a spectrum from narrative as reflecting or reporting on a pre-existing or essential Self to narrative constituting the Self. Writings at the former end of the spectrum understand narrative as a valuable way of gaining insight into the nature and workings of a Self that pre-exists any given narrative of that Self. To be sure, narrative might bring an order to experience that it otherwise might not have, but in this view of narrative the Self exists prior to, and independently of, narrative. This is what I have termed here the 'essentialist Self', reflecting an approach that claims to reflect with greater or lesser accuracy what the Self is 'really' like. At the other end of the spectrum we have the view that rather than reflecting an essential Self, narrative is the process whereby we constitute our Selves, our identities. Authors such as Schechtman (1996) argue that narrative is constitutive of the Self, that is, narrative is the way we understand ourselves, and without narrative there is no Self to understand. Schechtman (1996, p 101), in arguing the case for a narrative self-constitution view, puts it starkly:

> The differences between the kind of life led by an individual with a totally nonnarrative self-conception and the kind of life led by the rest of us [a narrative self-conception] are so pronounced and important that it does not seem like an exaggeration to say that the individuals who live such lives are not persons.

In what follows we discuss, first, the essentialist Self, and then, two forms of narrative constitution, the dialogic and the rhizomatic.

Essentialist Self

In this view the Self can be considered as a centred, individual subject that can be known, a central 'I' 'as a bounded, unique, more or less integrated motivational and cognitive universe; a dynamic center of awareness, emotion, judgment, and action organized into a distinctive whole and set contrastively both against other such wholes and against a social and natural background …' (Geertz, 1974, p 31). This is the I of Descartes' 'cogito ergo sum' and the Self of Locke who expresses it thus:

> … we must consider what a person stands for; which, I think, is a thinking, intelligent being, that has reason and reflection, and can consider itself, as itself, the same thinking thing in different times and places; which it does only by that consciousness which is inseparable from thinking and seems to be essential to it; it being impossible for any one to perceive without perceiving that he does perceive. (Locke, 1836/1964, pp 225-6)

This view of the Self as a being with frontiers, separate from others and with our own distinct personality, beliefs and attitudes, rests on the notion of continuity of identity, that the Self at one point in time is the same, at least in most significant respects, as the Self at another point in time. This view allows us to hold individuals accountable for past actions – this is the person who abused this child and this Self and no other should be held responsible, or that it is I and no other Self that should receive credit or compensation for my sacrifice or service (see Schechtman, 1996). This is the view of the Self that allows for temporary insanity, that is, a break in the continuity of the Self, to be used as a defence against legal and moral culpability.

Such departures from a normative Self form the basis for diagnosis of mental disorders, particularly diagnoses of personality disorders that are defined by experiences and behaviours that depart from cultural norms and expectations. The following is taken form a nursing text on mental disorders:

> [Paranoid personality] disorder is marked by conspicuous and persistent self-reference, that is the tendency to misinterpret the words and actions of others as having special significance for, and being directed against, self. Such persons may be excessively jealous, quarrelsome and litigious (inclined to engage in law suits) and may go to extreme lengths to avenge imagined injustices. Suspicion of others may be marked, and real or imagined grievances may be nursed and magnified for inordinate periods of time. Self-importance may be excessive and aggression is not uncommon. Feuds may be enthusiastically embarked upon with neighbours or colleagues at work. (Lyttle, 1986, p 377)

Here we see the paranoid personality being defined against an implicit normative Self, as indicated by trait modifiers such as *conspicuous and persistent* self-reference, *excessively* jealous, quarrelsome and litigious, going to *extreme* lengths, *excessive* self-importance and so on, the modifiers marking departures from everyday self-reference, jealousy, self-importance and so on.

The essentialist Self is also the notion of Self that lurks in the background when people say of their relative with dementia, 'He is not the person I married', or 'She is a shell of the person she used to be'. It is this Self the loss of which seems so frightening when faced with psychological disintegration. Indeed, the loss of certain capacities essential to personhood has prompted some authors, such as Brock (1993) and Harris (1985), to state that people with dementia lose personhood, the moral status that goes with being a Self defined in essentialist terms. An essentialist view of the Self also lies, often unarticulated, behind much of person-centred care and the personalisation agenda in health and social care with their emphasis on control, participation and the knowledge and aspirations of individuals that are to form the basis of service provision as in, for example, the government's policy document *Excellence and fairness* (Cabinet Office, 2008). (The relationship between narrative and social policy is explored in Chapter 5.)

In this view of the Self, narratives can perform a number of functions. First, they can be seen to reflect who this person is and are therefore a way to understand the individual. On the basis of what we learn from the stories that people tell about themselves and about others we can build up a picture of that person, identify their strengths and weaknesses, clarify desires and goals and develop appropriate plans to address difficulties. For example, through life history work dementia care practitioners may build up an idea of the individual on which they develop a person-centred care plan incorporating the desires, interests, values, relationships and so on that were meaningful and important to the individual prior to the onset and progression of the dementia (see, for example, Dementia UK, 2011). Similarly, a social worker might explore the roots of current difficulties, finding out about childhood trauma through the stories a service user might tell. Also, narratives can be used to present explanations and/or mitigating circumstances for departures from the essential Self – extreme stress might cause an otherwise mild-mannered individual to explode in anger, or an otherwise honest and law-abiding but poor parent shoplifts food in order to feed the children. In each of these scenarios there is a Self that is being reported on, either implicitly or explicitly.

The second function that narratives can perform in this view is to provide an over-arching framework for understanding one's life, in other words, understanding one's life as a coherent story. This is the sense of a Self that is following a particular path or direction in pursuit of goals, dreams or ambitions – it has an anticipated biography. This anticipated biography can, of course, be disrupted by any number of unforeseen events such as chronic illness (see Bury, 1982), trauma (Sandelowski, 1994), injury (Soklaridis et al, 2011), unemployment, divorce or loss (Ketokivi, 2008).

Biographical disruption, according to Ketokivi, disrupts the taken-for-granted assumptions about the future on which the anticipated narrative is founded, and thus forces people to rethink their biography and self-concept. Tekin (2011, p 365) describes this well in her discussion of the *Diagnostic and Statistical Manual*, arguing that on receiving a diagnosis of major depressive disorder a person may:

> ... redefine her past experiences based on the descriptive framework established by the diagnostic schema, reassess the psychological and historical facts of her life in the light of the theory underlying her diagnosis, start to reevaluate certain events of her past as earlier symptoms of her mental disorder, and so on. After being diagnosed, she may make better sense of, say, her increasing sadness, significant weight loss, insomnia, and suicidal thoughts exacerbated by feelings of hopelessness and despair in her early adulthood. This understanding may lead her to reassess her failure in her first job as an outcome of mental disorder, instead of, say, incompetence. The alteration in the subject's autobiographical narrative may generate changes in her future plans, hopes, desires, anticipations, expectations, habits, as well as her relationships with others.

Such biographical disruptions may be the initiating factor in bringing individuals, voluntarily or involuntarily, into the sphere of social services. Furthermore, while for some the intervention of social services might help ameliorate the difficulties presented by the disruption – for example, in maximising welfare benefits, accessing support services, developing alternative social networks and so on – for others, the intervention of social services might itself be biographically disruptive. In research I conducted on allegations of child abuse, the sudden appearance of social services threatened the parents' anticipated biography as normal, decent enough parents going about their everyday business as best they could in the face of worry and adversity (see Baldwin, 2006a, on the impact on the sense of Self following accusations of child abuse).

Whatever the benefits of the essentialist view of the Self, however, it is limited in both its application and its alignment with social work philosophy and values. It is limited in application in that it has little to say about how interactions with others shape the Self – interactions are simply meetings of already formed selves that react to other selves in a particular way and thus limit the possibility for the use of Self (see, for example, Heydt and Sherman, 2005; Mandell, 2007) as a means to foster change. It is limited in its alignment with social work philosophy and values because it assumes an underlying same-ness rather than difference and uniqueness, assumes that Self is a-social, a-historical and a-cultural in that political, social and cultural conventions and mores may have an impact on it (that is, the notions of a Self with defined frontiers, as a collection of characteristics and as an individual are not themselves socially constructed – see, for example, Morris, 1972, on the discovery of the individual). It also takes for granted the idea that divergence from the norms of the essential Self is problematic rather than the active construction of an alternative Self. Each of these assumptions conflicts with social work's commitment to understanding the dynamic of the individual in personal, social, cultural and political context and to the appreciation of uniqueness and promotion of diversity that we find in social work's code of practice.

Dialogical Self

If the problems with the essentialist Self are to be overcome, we need to look at ways of perceiving the Self in a more social and fluid way. We find this in notions of the dialogical Self in which the subject, the Self, is conceptualised as decentred and social. Salgado and Clegg (2011, p 424) note that 'Self–identity becomes a matter of socially situating oneself and negotiating with others one's own identity – the fixed Self becomes fluid, socially constituted, and unstable.' In this view, there is no central 'I' controlling or coordinating multiple aspects of an independent Self, but the subject is decentred in two ways. First, by comprising multiple 'I-s', each with its own voice, position and worldview at times in competition and conflict with other 'I-s', depending on the situation. This is the polyphonous or dialogical Self as put forward by Hermans et al (1992). The term 'polyphonous' is drawn from the work of Russian literary theorist Mikhail Bakhtin who, in discussing Dostoevsky's *The Brothers Karamazov*, argues that within the book there are multiple authors and perspectives and not simply that of Dostoevsky himself. Within this framework, there is not a single inner, coherent Self but a 'multiplicity of worlds, with each world having its own author telling a story relatively independent of the authors of the other worlds' (Hermans et al, 1992, p 28). For example, I am, at one and the same time, an academic, a social worker, a teacher, a learner, a researcher, a friend, a husband, a human companion to a dog, a brother, a son, an uncle, a car driver, a consumer, an anarchist, vegan, Catholic and so on. Each of these has a voice and may '… agree, disagree, understand, misunderstand, oppose, contradict, question, challenge and even ridicule the I in another position' (Hermans, 2002, p 249).

The second way in which the Self might be considered decentred is in understanding the Self as heteroglossic, another term drawn from Bakhtin. The term 'heteroglossia' again refers to the multiplicity of voices but, in contrast to polyphony which emphasises the different voices of different selves interacting as equals, the heteroglossic perspective positions the Self within the diversity of social contexts that operate in, and other Selves that populate, any culture or society. In the heteroglossic perspective the diverse, multiple discourses that push and pull against each other in society are uniquely configured in the peculiar utterances of the individual, thus capturing, fleetingly, the incessant interaction between the speaking person and the linguistic and social contexts within which s/he is communicating. Cresswell and Baerveldt (2011, p 264), identifying more with this perspective, take issue with Herman's understanding of the dialogical Self, arguing that he does not adequately account for the 'embodied' or social relations that shape the Self, neglecting 'the social quality of lived embodied experience.' As they otherwise put it, 'Dialogue … needs to be understood as expressive of the juxtaposition of personally experienced social corporeality, and this grants us a richer role of sociality beyond that of intersubjective exchange' (p 272). In both ways of decentring the Self, there are no linear, coherent narratives coordinated by the 'I' as in the essentialist Self, but a limitless possibility of multiple narratives unendingly shaped by social, cultural and historical factors.

This way of viewing the Self captures the dynamic between the individual and her/his context. Just as Tess in Hardy's *Tess of the d'Urbervilles* cannot be known outside of the social and moral conventions of Victorian Britain or Caspar Hauser known save as the object of the desires, ambitions or scepticism of others (see Wasserman, 1985), we cannot know or understand ourselves without accounting for the shaping influences of family, friends, community and society, and in so appreciating those influences we are able to approach others in their diversity and uniqueness. A dialogical approach to Self, then, seems more attuned with the expressed commitments of social work to understanding the individual within networks of influences and can find expression in social work approaches such as psychodynamics, systems theory or the more radical/structural end of Marxist social work as expressed by Leonard (1984), and the varying narratives of those involved become the raw material with which to work with service users to identify presenting issues, preferred outcomes and possible solutions. This is so whether one is working with families toward shared resolutions of accepted difficulties or individually as an advocate for the service user in the face of competing and potentially oppressive narratives.

There are, however, limitations to both Hermans' and Cresswell and Baerveldt's understandings of the dialogical Self. The first, put forward by Hermans, identifies an internal dialogical positioning which, while allowing for a multiplicity of 'I' stances, does not take into consideration the undeniable and incalculable effects of social relations. This is well illustrated by the 2006 documentary *Zidane: A 21st century portrait*, in which the football player Zinedine Zidane is the focus of the filmmakers. He alone is consecutively followed as he passes, attempts to score, talks to his teammates and scratches his head. The audience sees him without any context, however, as we never see with whom he is communicating or for what purposes – he is more or less completely isolated on the field (Gordon and Parreno, 2006).

The second, as developed by Cresswell and Baerveldt, puts the Self entirely in the realm of social context, without allocating it any agentive capacity. This is the character Zelig in Woody Allen's 1983 film of the same name who morphs into the body types, speech patterns and behaviours of the people around him, a human chameleon entirely shaped by his social circumstances. Zelig therefore offers a representation of Cresswell and Baerveldt's socially constituted Self in which Zelig's Self quite literally embodies all of his social interactions and relationships. In Zidane and in Zelig neither person can be understood in his entirety as only half of the picture dominates at a given moment.

The problem of the dialogical Self then becomes how to account for an agentive Self that is also socially and relationally shaped. Graham Harman offers one possibility for reconciling these positions in his discussion of object–oriented philosophy when he argues that 'the object is deeper than any possible relations to it' (Latour et al, 2011, p 37). As he says elsewhere, 'Objects exist as autonomous units, but they also exist in conjunction with their qualities, accidents, relations, and moments without being reducible to these' (Harman, 2009, p 156). There is thus what we may call a 'thingness' in all objects that is influenced by, but not fully reducible to, social relations. In contrast to the essentialist Self that posits a commanding central 'I' acting forcefully on its environments, we have instead a dialogical Self with a multiplicity of Self positions unarguably produced by social processes.

For the purposes of social work, the dialogical Self provides a much better starting point for realising both the uniqueness of the individual and their constitutive social contexts (see, for example, van Nijnattan, 2007) and for developing practice based on this (see, for example, Yan and Wong, 2005, on the development of cultural competence). It also points to a narrative mode of being not confined by one meta–narrative but free to fashion, create, invent and discover on a continual basis. Indeed, this is the basis of narrative therapy – see White and Epston (1990); Freedman and Combs (1996); Abels and Abels (2001). The idea that an object (human or non–human) cannot be exhausted simply by accounting for its relationships, combined with dialogism's positing of a fundamentally relational Self, opens the door for a discussion of the rhizomatic Self, a Self that expands its constitutive possibilities even further creating limitless opportunities for narratively understanding the Self.

Rhizomatic Self

Social work, I have suggested, is founded on a concern for the uniqueness of the Other and the nature of the relationship between the Self and the Other. In so doing we need to somehow bring together an agentic Self capable of acting in the world in ways not solely determined by its surroundings and the shaping influences and forces that curtail the egoistic spontaneity of the Self (Levinas, 1961). We can do this, I believe, through incorporating the Deleuzo-Guattarian concepts of becoming, de-territorialisation, rhizomatics and lines of flight.

Deleuze and Guattari (1987) take issue with Western ways of thinking, acting and knowing that have emerged since the Enlightenment. For them, such structures of thought are linear, hierarchical/vertical, fixed and deeply rooted – structures they characterise as arborescent (tree-like). In this light the arborescent Self can be seen as emerging from the Enlightenment possessive individualism of Locke and Hume to a humanistic conceptualisation of Self as individual self-ownership, rooted in that individual's history and personality, consistent and internally and externally coherent and framed within a socio-legal discourse of rights and citizenship, and in this we can see the affinities of the arborescent Self with the essentialist Self discussed earlier.

For Deleuze and Guattari, a discourse of the Self that demands unity, order, coherence, hierarchy and linearity is a form of arborescence which constructs the Self within three strata: organism, significance and subjectification. The first points to the necessity to be organised as a body, the second to being interpreted through hierarchical language and the third to the requirement to become a clearly identifiable, singular Self (see Markula, 2006, for a fuller discussion of these strata). These three strata operate to construct a defined, stable identity related to fixed categories such as class, 'race' or gender (or other binary distinctions) or in other constructions such as patient, client or service user where such categories serve to define how those so labelled may be perceived, related to and treated. So, for example, in the case study in Chapter 6 the mother was framed as uncooperative or awkward as a result of, among other things, refusing to meet social workers in her own home, insisting on communication in writing, fax and email, wanting to record meetings and insisting that the social workers adhere to the policies and procedures laid down by the local authority and challenging them when they did not; thus she failed to fit into the stereotypical (and required) service user identity as compliant with the social workers' definitions of the situation and the social work process and as less articulate, knowledgeable and perceptive than the social workers themselves.

In contrast rhizomes are non-linear, horizontal, non-centred, anarchic and nomadic. Rhizomes are defined by their connections rather than their roots and spread horizontally across time and space. Unlike trees rhizomes do not have a defining form – they can take any shape or direction and nodes can be connected to any other nodes. Transposing this image to how the Self might be conceived we have an image that is one of multiplicity:

> This vision – the narrative self as a postmodern story – is related to the postmodern idea that the self has no stable core but is multiple, multivoiced, discontinuous, and fragmented…. From this viewpoint, the self is not something that is inherently given, is fixed, or has one core. On the contrary, the self can be compared with "a buzzing beehive so agile and inconsistent, we can barely keep track of it" (Rosseel, 2001). (Sermijn et al, 2008, p 637)

This Self defies subjectification, that is, the requirement for a clearly defined, singular identity (see Markula, 2006). Furthermore, the Self can be seen as in process, a becoming through connectedness. It does not rest at or in any particular node of the rhizome but travels the spaces between such nodes.

This notion of becoming is also central to the work of Deleuze and Guattari who argue that rhizomes are the outcome of struggle between 'lines of articulation' and 'lines of flight'. Lines of articulation seek to establish unity, coherence and stability through the setting of rules, establishing explanations, ordering and categorising and defining centre–periphery relations. One needs only examine standard social work texts to see how such lines of articulation are presented as the crux of good social work practice, from assessment and eligibility criteria to care planning and review (see, for example, Parker and Bradley, 2010). The processes of articulation establish the Self through framing individuals as conforming to the demands and expectations of ordered classifications such as 'heterosexual parent', 'good employee' and 'effective manager', or, for our purposes here, the 'difficult to engage service user'. While social work generally has a reasonable record in supporting difference, we need to examine what lines of articulation we support or promote and for what reason. It may be that we do not want to support and promote a paedophilic identity and can give good reason for not doing so. However, can we do the same for someone who wishes to become an amputee or someone who forms an identity around anorexia as a lifestyle choice? The majority of professional literature on this subject seems to take the form of a line of articulation that denies the acceptability of such a desire through the psychologisation of that desire into body integrity identity disorder. Similarly, how many social workers would encourage someone to seek support from a pro-Ana website to help them achieve their goals of being thin? (See, for example, de Souza Ramos et al, 2011, on the cultural identity supported by pro-Ana virtual communities.)

Less controversially, perhaps, we can see another 'line of articulation' in Kitwood's (1997) notion of person-centred dementia care with its focus on the 'person behind the dementia' and the range of practices that have arisen to protect and maintain that person from the ravages of dementia – life history, reminiscence, psychotherapy, maintaining previous relationships, interests and activities and so on. Such person–centred care posits a Self that is in some (unarticulated) way related to memory, relationships and past behaviours that can be, through skilful management, protected and maintained. In so doing such care seeks to establish, or more accurately reproduce, the unity, coherence and stability of the Self that it posits as being behind the dementia – and is thus an arborescent conception of the Self.

Lines of flight, on the other hand, seek to make connections across borders, disrupt established lines of articulation, dissemble unity and coherence and thus open up possibilities for becoming Other and for multiplicities (becoming variegated others). We can see these lines of flight reflected in developments such as queer theory that contests essentialist and heteronormative categories of identity, asserting that identity is multiplicitous and ever-changing, never reducible to a fixed essence (Butler, 1989); crip theory which transforms '… the substantive, material uses to which queer/disabled existence has been put by a system of compulsory able-bodiedness … [and] imagining bodies and desires otherwise' (McRuer, 2006, p 32); or the experimentations of Australian performance artist Stelarc who challenges notions of fixedness in arborescent thinking by breaking down traditional conceptualisations of the unity and stability of the body through performances such as his third, mechanical arm project or the grafting of a third ear onto his arm (see Gibson and Smith, 2005). We see such multiplicities in narratives of transgender where the binary models of fe/male are contested as individuals attempt to define for themselves who they are, defying not only traditional gender categories but also a unified transgender identity (see, for example, Haynes and MacKenna, 2001; Hines, 2006).

Lines of flight, or rhizomatics, focus on multiplicities, and in terms of the Self this means seeing the Self as a process of becoming through association with, and relationship to, the world and Others (see Goodley, 2007a, for a discussion of rhizomatic parenthood). The Self is thus fluid, contingent and dynamic, a process or performative act made real (or unreal) in each and every interaction. This Self is the basis for the narrative ethics that I discuss in Chapter 4 and in Part III of the book we explore how the Self is constructed by various narratives – those of the meta-narratives of disability, the construction of the dangerous mother in cases of alleged child abuse and the compromised Self in much of the discourse on mental health/disorder.

Self and self-reflection

I end this chapter with a short reflection on the importance of the concept of the Self for social work and social workers. The approaches to understanding the Self discussed in this chapter may be helpful in working with service users. Understanding how service users see themselves and how they are seen by others is important in assessing the situation, identifying areas on which to work, finding resources on which to draw and so on. We may want to work with some service users to develop an enhanced sense of Self so as to garner strength to counter oppressive situations or attempted impositions of undesirable identities; with others we might want to help generate a collective identity from which individuals can gain social and emotional support; with still others we might want to help maintain identity in changing circumstances such as following the loss of a close relative or the move into residential care. Without knowing who our service users are, we are incapable of developing the proper relationship that will help them.

But this is only one side of the story – we also need to understand who we are, the stories that we tell about ourselves, the stories that influence us, the identities that we are called on to perform. For example, different roles and expectations of social work over time have demanded changes in identity (see Passarinho, 2008) – in the UK from an historical paternalistic approach through the professional case manager of the 1970s and 1980s to the more consumer-oriented approach of the 1990s and the new managerialism of the late 20th and early 21st century. Understanding who we are, how we are shaped by socio-cultural-political forces and how we negotiate multiple identities helps us approach others in creative, rhizomatic ways. This is an extension of the argument put forward by Miehls and Moffat (2000) who argue convincingly for the exploration of Self in dialogical terms – that is, for a Self understood in its social relations. I suggest that we need also, if we are to understand our social work identity(ies), to take into account relations with physical and structural factors – for example, how the hierarchical organisation of the workplace might have an impact on our sense of Self. Having worked in hierarchical organisations, in 'flat' teams and as a member of a collective, I have come to appreciate how these have affected how I see myself – as employee, colleague and comrade.

In my classes I encourage social work students to explore narrative through self-reflection, using tools from self-development classes and auto-ethnography, that is, performing analysis of the personal in order to understand cultural experience (see Ellis et al, 2011). In understanding ourselves in our social, political, cultural context and in our personal uniqueness, I suggest, we are better able to understand and empathise with others. This is a deeper self-understanding than that provided by being self-reflective (in Miehls and Moffatt's [2000] conceptualisation of this) in that it seeks to locate and understand our Selves in dynamic interaction with a landscape populated not only by humans but non-humans and discourses as well. In effect, it is applying the same form of assessment to ourselves as we would to service users.

Further reflections

This chapter has focused on the first level of narrativity, that concerning the individual – how the stories we tell and those that are told about us shape who we are. This conception of Self is, I think, more in line with social work's stated values. Social workers implicitly carry with them certain views about the Self and how it is fashioned and maintained, and it is therefore important to understand the implications of these views for interacting with the service user. The social worker's ideas about the main aspects of the Self not only influence their personal and professional impressions of the service user; they also affect assessment procedures and intervention decisions.

In the exploration of Self in this chapter I have described three positions on narrative and the Self, ultimately advocating a conception that supports a Self unconstrained by normative dictates about how the Self should be shaped or what path it should follow. Narrative has great potential here, operating as a constitutive force in self-formation and thereby offering unlimited means of becoming. This means that an essentialist notion of Self should be abandoned in favour of this more contextual, narrative understanding of the Self as socially involved, non-linear and, in Deleuzian terms, rhizomatic.

4

Social work ethics and narrative

It is my contention that whatever the merits of BASW's *Code of ethics* there are problems aligning what is basically an abstract principlist approach with what is essentially a concrete, narrative activity. In other words, there are two fundamental mis-alignments – one philosophical, one practical – between the Association's values and its ethical framework. The philosophical mis-alignment rests in the promotion of an essentially normative ethics for a socially and culturally diverse world, the two relying on competing and incompatible epistemologies. The practical mis-alignment lies in the attempt to corral ethical conduct into adherence to a set of pronouncements, thus removing ethical creativity and personal responsibility for the uniqueness of the ethical encounter. What appears on the surface as clear, coherent and practically useful is, on closer examination, quite the opposite.

In this chapter I attempt three things. First, to justify the bold statements made in the opening paragraph. I do this by interrogating the *Code of ethics* close association with principlism as found in biomedical ethics, chiefly in the work of Beauchamp and Childress (2001), and the Code's uncritical reliance on deontology. Second, I argue that social work requires an ethics that is aligned with its fundamental values. I attempt this by reflecting on the work of Levinas and Deleuze and Guattari, and how these continental philosophers can provide a more coherent philosophical underpinning for social work ethics than either principlism or deontology. Finally, I outline an ethics founded in and expressed through narrative as being more appropriate for the social work enterprise.

The first, and most obvious, point to make about the BASW *Code of ethics* is that it is explicitly principle-driven. In Section 4 of the Code it clearly states that guidance on ethical practice is given 'by applying the values and principles set out above to the principal areas of social work practice.' In the earlier part of the Code five fundamental social work values are presented: of human dignity and worth, social justice, service to humanity, integrity and competence. Each of these values is followed by a list of principles designed to uphold that particular value. So, for instance, the value of human rights is upheld by the following six principles:

- Respect basic human rights as expressed in the UN UDHR and other international conventions derived from that Declaration.
- Show respect for all persons, and respect service users' beliefs, values, culture, goals, needs, preferences, relationships and affiliations.
- Safeguard and promote service users' dignity, individuality, rights, responsibilities and identity.

- Foster individual well-being and autonomy, subject to due respect for the rights of others.
- Respect service users' rights to make informed decisions, and ensure that service users and carers participate in decision-making processes.
- Ensure the protection of service users, which may include setting appropriate limits and exercising authority, with the objective of safeguarding them and others.

If we examine the principles for each of the values it is notable that many fit with the four principles of bioethics, in substance if not in exact terminology. The four principles are:

- Autonomy: 'self-rule that is free from both controlling interference by others and from limitations, such as inadequate understanding, that prevent meaningful choice. The autonomous individual acts freely in accordance with a self-chosen plan ...' (Beauchamp and Childress, 2001, p 58).
- Beneficence: '... refers to an action done to benefit others', and this principle 'establishes an obligation to help others further their important and legitimate interests' (p 166).
- Non-maleficence: the obligation not to inflict harm on others in the 'non-normative sense of thwarting, defeating or setting back some party's interests' (p 116).
- Justice: 'fair, equitable, and appropriate treatment in light of what is due or owed to persons' (p 226), which includes distributive justice, referring to the distribution of rights and responsibilities in society, and material justice, referring to resources to meet fundamental needs (pp 227-8).

The links between the bioethical principlist framework of Beauchamp and Childress and the provisions of the BASW *Code of ethics* are clear. For example, social workers' duties to foster individual well-being and autonomy (para 3.1.2.d), respect service users' rights to make informed decisions and ensure that service users and carers participate in decision-making processes (para 3.1.2.e) all relate closely to the principle of autonomy; duties to place service users' needs and interests before their own beliefs, aims, views and advantage (para 3.4.2.a) and ensuring the protection of service users (para 3.1.2.f) and using their power and authority in ways which serve humanity (para 3.3.2.c) relate to beneficence; duties to avoid any behaviour which may violate professional boundaries, result in unintentional harm or damage the professional relationship (para 3.4.2.f) and to minimise the risk of conflict, exploitation or harm in all relationships with current or former service users (para 3.4.2.g) address the principle of non-maleficence; and the duties to promote social fairness and the equitable distribution of resources within their work, aiming to minimise barriers and expand choice and potential for all service users, especially those who are disadvantaged, vulnerable or oppressed, or who have exceptional needs (para 3.2.2.c), clearly accord with the principle of justice (references to the provisions of the *Code of ethics*, BASW, 2002). While these are examples, it is possible, I think, to assign most, if not all, of the principles listed under the first four values of the Code (human dignity and worth, social justice, service to humanity and integrity) to one or other of the four principles of bioethics, and it is not surprising that key textbooks on social work ethics (for example, Banks, 2006; Parrott, 2010) allocate much space to the discussion of a principlist framework for ethics.

Underpinning this principlist approach to ethics is a reliance on duty, rules and obligation, namely, deontology. This is reflected in the fact that each of the sections on principles in the Code is prefaced with the words 'Social workers have a duty to', a preface followed by a list of do's and don'ts ranging from rather vague calls to 'use their power and authority in ways which serve humanity' to specific proscriptions against intimate or sexual conduct with current service users. Furthermore, the Code seeks to bind social workers to compliance by introducing rules requiring the promotion and upholding of the Code itself and rules concerning private conduct that might contravene professional principles and standards or which damage the profession's integrity and promoting and upholding the Code itself. In other words, it is the duty of the social worker to uphold the duty of the social worker – presumably to infinite regress.

This way of thinking about ethics has a number of problems. A number of these are problems with principlist and deontological approaches generally, and a number are heightened by, if not specific to, social work.

With regard to the general problems of deontology and principlism, there are three significant issues. First, there is the problem of conflicting duties or principles. Neither deontology nor principlism argue for a hierarchy of duties or principles and so can offer little guidance as to practical action when duties or principles pull in opposite directions. Two examples: where a service user's best interest clashes with a social worker's responsibility to his or her workplace, whose interests should take precedence? Or the very obvious clash between autonomy and best interests involved in detaining a service user against their will under mental health legislation.

The second problem with deontological and principlist approaches to ethics is that they take a normative stance as to those duties and principles they embrace. Indeed, the principlist approach in bioethics is celebrated by some authors precisely for this reason. Principlism, according to Gillon (1994), provides universal, simple, accessible and culturally neutral principles that embrace a common set of moral commitments, cluster together a common set of moral issues and generate a common moral language. The BASW *Code of ethics* seeks to do the same – to provide a common framework to which social workers can (and must) commit themselves and ways of identifying and resolving ethical issues in practice. While principlism has the benefit of providing consistency and a reasonably secure base for professional practice, it constrains ethical thinking to those problems that can be framed within principlism, promotes uniformity in ethical thinking and reduces ethics to a checklist of principles (Harris, 2003).

The Code does try to address this problem by providing modifiers to what would be, without such modifiers, too firmly categorical statements. Indeed, the ethical practice guidance that forms the latter part of the Code abounds with such modifiers as 'whenever possible', 'as much as possible', 'exceptional circumstances', 'where appropriate', 'acceptable', 'requisite', 'suitable' and so on. The effect of such modifiers is to undermine the normative nature of the rules that are being put forward as interpretation of such modifiers is subjective enough to allow for almost any action to be ethically justified under one or other elements of the Code.

Related to this problem of normativity is social work's commitment to promote culturally appropriate practice and culturally sensitive services, an aim that seems to be contradicted by the commitment to a universalist ethics. Walker (2009) has convincingly argued that principlism fails in two significant ways. First, 'principlism simply cannot capture the moral norms that are part of the common morality' (p 230) – giving the example of bestiality as an immoral act not covered by principlism – and that to be able to capture common morality other principles such as respect and purity are necessary. Second, that there are *community-specific* norms that are obligatory for members of those communities but they are not universal. Indeed, Evans (2000) has argued that principlism is a peculiarly Western form of ethical reasoning, and Ryan (2004, p 159) has said that it 'is drawn principally from Western philosophical traditions (indebted, in particular, to Kantian deontology and utilitarianism) and developed within institutional settings of the West and in light of European and North American legal and regulatory frameworks.' The tension here is between social work's commitment to culturally appropriate and sensitive practice and its reliance on a Western 'universalist' ethics.

Third, while social work is concerned with the person, principlism as an ethical framework has no explicit concept of the person or personhood. Rather, the individual with whom principlism is concerned is both implicit and abstract, ultimately framed within the confines of individual autonomy. As we have seen in Chapter 3, this essentialist view of the person is limited and unable to capture the multiple Self or the notion of becoming. It is not surprising, therefore, that key principlist texts such as Beauchamp and Childress' *Principles of biomedical ethics* have nothing to say about personhood or the Self. Thus we have social work claiming to have at its centre the individual person in context but relying on an abstract person-less ethics.

If social work is to realise its values and principles as outlined in the *Code of ethics*, it is essential, in my view, that it has an ethical framework that aligns with those values and principles. In other words, it needs an ethical framework that focuses on a dynamic rather than essentialist Self, on difference and uniqueness rather than abstract homogeneity, on emergence and becoming rather than stasis. This framework, I believe, can be founded in the work of Emmanuel Levinas, particularly around the relationship of the Self and the Other and, drawing on the work of Deleuze and Guattari (see Chapter 3), finds an appropriate expression in narrative ethics.

Levinas, the Self and the Other

Levinas' approach to ethics (see Levinas, 1961) is distinctly different to that of principlism in that he argues that ethics is, fundamentally, a unique relationship between the Self (or, for our purposes, the social worker) and the Other (again, the service user). This relationship is marked by difference and a recognition that the Other cannot be reduced to the Self as the Self and Other are completely separate, radically different entities. This is what Levinas terms alterity.

Levinas, like Deleuze and Guattari, conceives of the Self as a unique, but not fixed, entity that experiences the world with pleasure and interest (Davis, 1996, p 43). The Self assumes itself to be both powerful and free but this power and freedom, this egoistic spontaneity, is called into question when the Self comes into contact with the Other and is no longer in unique possession of the world. The encounter with the Other disrupts the egoistic power and freedom of the Self and forces certain unavoidable decisions on the Self. The Self can attempt to impose itself onto the Other by insisting on the correctness, applicability and acceptance of its worldview, interpretations, concepts, definitions, beliefs, attitudes and behaviours; or the Self can alternatively respond with a sense of responsibility and obligation toward the Other in all her/his alterity (see Schotsmans, 1999). The former response is, according to Levinas, an act of violence and, for Robbins, responding to the uniqueness and alterity of the Other using a set of a priori moral principles is just such an act.

The Self must, therefore, come to terms with the alterity of the Other, and this, for Levinas, is the site of ethics: 'The strangeness of the Other, his irreducibility to the I, to my thoughts and my possessions, is precisely accomplished as a calling into question of my spontaneity, as ethics' (Levinas, quoted in Davis, 1996, p 36). To describe it another way, the ethical experience with the Other involves looking into the vulnerability that characterises the Other's Face with our prior assumptions of our own power, and realising that the call of the vulnerable Other, as it is expressed in the Face, is ultimately a plea, 'Do not kill me' (see Benso, 1996; Schotsmans, 1999). As social workers we carry with us many assumptions of our own power, efficacy and necessity as professionals that act to disable service users and others (see, for example, Illich et al, 1977, on professionalised need). Welfare institutions such as health and education, according to Illich (1975, 1976, 1977), undermine the ability of individuals and groups to define their own needs and decide on how those needs will be met by insisting on the consumption of their professionalised services. In effect, this is applying a singular model to the expanse of difference and, metaphorically, killing the Other, who may wish to seek her/his own pathway in these matters. (For further elaboration of how professions disable Others, see McKnight, 1995.)

The encounter with the Face does not have to result in violence, however, and can provide us with the opportunity to become truly human, as it is in this encounter that the good of the Self and the Other converge. Sokolowski's (1989, p 269) phrasing of this matter, although made with regard to medicine, could easily apply to social work: '… in the important arts, and specifically in the art of medicine, the goodness of the art will help shape the character of the person who practices it, because it will form him into someone who seeks the good of another as his own good. It will help the physician to be excellent not just as a doctor but as a human being.' In other words, the good practice of social work will shape us not only as good social workers but also as good people – our fate is tied up inextricably to our relationship with our service users.

Furthermore, given the uniqueness of the ethical encounter – that is, the encounter between this unique Self and this unique Other, at this time, in this place and under these circumstances – the Self and the Other are opened up to a multiplicity of possibilities. This multiplicity is what Deleuze and Guattari (1987) call 'lines of flight' (see Chapter 3), in which human beings are not tied to fixed patterns of being, but are free to construct and re-construct themselves in accordance with desire and in response to their circumstances. This can occur over the entire trajectory of a person's life; therefore, 'becoming' is a never-ending task, one that is continually stimulated when the Self meets the Other, and vice versa. Difference, emergence, multiplicity and interdependency – key concerns raised by Levinas and Deleuze and Guattari – are also key concerns of social work and as such need to be embedded within an ethical framework for social work. It is my argument that we can find such a framework in narrative ethics.

Narrative ethics

Before I present that argument, however, I want to make clear what I mean by narrative ethics as the term is used in the literature in a number of ways.

When discussing narrative in the Introduction I suggested that it is possible to take weaker or stronger positions on how narrative can be applied to understanding the world. The weaker positions, I suggested, were those that used narrative as an adjunct, as a means to support and enhance understandings framed by other primary concepts. The strong position, in contrast, is that which uses narrative as the lens through which to understand and explain the matter in hand, whether that be what it means to be 'Self' or how facts are constructed. In the field of ethics, a similar divide can be identified between those who use narrative in the service of another ethical framework and those who take narrative to be an ethical framework in and of itself. Within the former, three main positions can be identified: first, those who enrol narrative in the form of literature as a means of enhancing moral sensitivity and moral education (see, for example, Charon, 1994; Charon et al, 1995; Gregory, 2009); second, those who see the practice of writing as a means of enhancing empathy, sensitivity and understanding as well as the relationship and emotional connection with others (see, for example, Shapiro and Rucker, 2003; DasGupta and Charon, 2004); and third, those who elicit narratives as a means of gathering rich data on which to base ethical decision-making within whatever ethical framework is being used.

The strong position on narrative ethics views them as inextricably intertwined. It is more than listening to and recognising and analysing the features of important stories and then reacting to these in the social work intervention in accordance with the *Code of ethics*. With Hauerwas (1977) we advocate narrative as an essential part of ethical reasoning, saying that stories are vital for critical awareness and moral understanding. Hauerwas notes that 'Stories ... help us, as we hold them, to relate to our world.... So in allowing ourselves to adopt and be adopted by a particular story, we are in fact assuming a set of practices which will shape the ways we relate to our world...' (1977, p 36). As he points out, this approach offers much more flexibility and attentiveness to individual contexts than principlism. For Newton (1995, p 8),

> ... narrative ethics can be construed in two directions at once – on the one hand, as attributing to narrative discourse some kind of ethical status, and on the other, as referring to the way ethical discourse often depends on narrative structures – makes this reciprocity between narrative and ethics appear even more essential, more grammatical, so to speak, and less the accident of coinage.

Narrative is both the story being told and the telling of that story – the Said and the Saying, in Newton's words. This twofold nature embraces a twofold ethics: an ethics that is integral to the story being told, and an ethics of how that story is told, an ethics of the Said and an ethics of the Saying, of the narrated and the narrating.

This strong position incorporates six aspects of narrative that, taken together, provide a foundation for a narrative ethic. First, the strong relationship between narrative and the Self (see Chapter 3) brings together both a concern for a workable method and a concern for personhood. Unlike other ethical frameworks such as principlism, narrative links action with a sense of Self and character and is thus very much in line with Levinas' description of the meeting of Self and Other. If the Self is narrative in nature and encounters other Selves, again narrative in nature, it is reasonable to see those encounters as also being narrative in nature. Also, if the encounter between the Self and Other is inherently an ethical encounter, then it follows that the narrative encounter must also be ethical.

Second, narrative is concrete and unique and can accommodate considerable degrees of alterity both in content and form – witness for example, the range of subject matter, genres and form in literature, ranging from the very highly structured works of Poe to the meanderings of Tristram Shandy. Postmodern narratives, in particular, can embrace heterogeneity, non-linearly organised time and causality and space that is in motion and lacks a central point (see, for example Calvino, 1981; Sermijn et al, 2008). This focus on uniqueness and alterity is fundamentally aligned with the values and principles of social work promoted by BASW and its ambitions of culturally appropriate practice and cultural sensitivity.

Third, narrative is concerned with meanings as much as, if not more than, historical fact. Authors such as Spence (1982) argue that narrative has its own truth that stands on its own, regardless of whether it is consistent with what is thought to be historical truth. Thus attention to narrative is not about getting more accurate information but about ensuring that whatever assessment or intervention is undertaken is in accord with the meaning system of the service user and that there may be a trade-off between narrative and historical truth in the pursuit of enabling service users to live well, avoiding fixing their identity and respecting personhood (see, for example, the experiences of mental health service users in Cohen's study, 2008).

Fourth, narratives are contingent and fluid, flexible and dynamic. There is nothing inherent within a story that has to be that way as stories can always be rewritten. This allows for the possibility of more positive stories to be told, as, for example, in the practice of narrative therapy (see, for example, White and Epston, 1990; Freedman and Combs, 1996).

Fifth, in the process of co-construction or co-authoring of narrative one expresses solidarity with the Other. The process of co-construction pays close attention to the meanings, intentions, desires, goals, beliefs, background, thoughts and actions of the individual seeking help. The narrative social worker seeks to work within the individual's narrative framework to construct a mutually acceptable, credible and ultimately liveable narrative. This is not to abandon one's own morality in favour of the ethics of the Other, which is, in the words of Diedrich et al (2006, p 48), to become 'a passive listener to her ethical appeals and then a slave to her arbitrary bidding' – the danger identified by Hassan in Noddings' (1995) ethics of care (Hassan, 2008) – but to ensure that one uses one's own knowledge, skills, insights and morality in the service of the Other. In this way both the Self and the Other are cared for.

Finally, as narrative operates at different levels – individual, familial, community, society and discoursal (see Chapter 1) – it is uniquely aligned with the social work enterprise that requires respect for individuals, the recognition of diversity and individual, family, group and community differences, the promotion of human rights and the challenging of discriminatory or oppressive behaviour, policies and practices (see Chapter 2). Wilks (2005) echoes this when he argues that narrative ethics in social work has the capacity to take into account such issues as gender, culture, and so on that universalist frameworks such as principlism simply cannot.

If I have made the case for a narrative ethics it is now important to at least outline what such an ethics might look like. In particular I address four aspects of narrative that are essential to ethics: maintaining narrative agency, establishing the emergent plot, a sensitivity to, and an appreciation of, narrative webs and the accumulation of narrative resources.

Maintaining narrative agency

Maintaining narrative agency is probably the most straightforward aspect of a narrative ethics in that it translates relatively easily into obvious practical activities. At root, narrative agency is having the ability and opportunity to author one's own story, and there are ways in which social workers can facilitate this through advocacy or community work (see, for example, Chapter 2 on narratives of social justice). Even when service users might be narratively compromised through, for example, dementia or other conditions (and many of my examples will be from the field of dementia on the grounds that these are transferable to those without cognitive impairment, while the same might not be true the other way around), it is possible to create the conditions whereby narrative agency continues even when direct authorship is no longer possible:

- simply providing people with the opportunities to offer their narratives: for example, making space in our busy days to talk with people with dementia, by facilitating communication through such things as Talking Mats® (Murphy et al, 2005) and more overtly, by eliciting their stories through reminiscence projects (see, for example, Schweitzer and Bruce, 2008) and even psychotherapy (Cheston et al, 2003);
- narrativising other means of symbolic expression such as art, music and dance (see, for example Downs et al, 2006, who draw attention to the communicative possibilities of sound, music, behavioural cues and mirroring);
- attention to small stories that do not rely on extended communication (see Bamberg, 2004), that is, the micro-scale interactions between individuals that occur throughout the day. These can indicate, if we are open to their possibilities, facets of identity, agency and creativity on which narrative agency is based;
- engaging with people in the co-construction of their stories, and allowing them to become co-authors of our own (see, for example, Keady and Williams, 2005; Baldwin, 2006b).

Establishing the emergent plot

When individuals come to social services they are often in troubled and troubling states, states in which their normal, everyday narrative has ceased to function or make sense. In need of some assistance in establishing a new plot, service users are akin to the six people in Pirandello's *Six characters in search of an author* (1921/1998) who see themselves as incomplete because the writer of the play in which they were characters has died and there is no one to continue the story. These six characters approach the manager of a company of actors, asking whether he will be their author, so that, like Sancho Panza and Don Abbondio, they might have 'the fortune to find a fecundating matrix, a fantasy which could raise and nourish them: make them live for ever!'

Social workers may facilitate this by helping to provide a framework for the emerging plot, the direction in which the service user wants the story to go, how best to effect that navigation and the identification of resources to enable that narrative to be realised. This is a setting of a trajectory (perhaps based on what has gone before but not necessarily so) so that the emergent story makes sense. An applicable metaphor would be a loose script and plot within which the actors could ad lib according to the dynamics of the situation, although each is charged with the responsibility of moving the plot forward. We see this process admirably achieved in Tim Burton's *Big fish* (Burton, 2003) in the final scenes where Edward Bloom (played by Albert Finney) lies dying. He is visited by his son, Will, from whom he has been somewhat estranged over the years due to Will's perception of his father as an insincere fraud. This perception is based on Edward's tendency to tell elaborate and bizarre tales about his life – for example, running off to the circus with Carl the Giant, escaping from Korea in the company of conjoined twins. In the final scenes of the movie Edward is only partly conscious and is unable to continue his story, so he asks Will to tell him the ending. Although lacking the narrative accomplishment of his father, Will tells the story of him and his father escaping from hospital and making their way down to the river where Edward is greeted by people from his life. Will carries his father into the river and on lowering him into the water, Edward morphs into a big fish and swims away.

In terms of social work, the establishment of a mutually acceptable plot may involve elements that are in line with a person's previous narrative, thus validating that previous narrative (that all is not lost), but may also create new openings – the 'thrill of narrative freedom' (Gullette, 2004) – by steering service users away from the negative features of a previous narrative and helping them find, if not a meaning, at least a way of facing the oncoming challenges (a quest narrative). Working with those who misuse alcohol would be an example of this, where narratives of excessive drinking are replaced by more constructive narratives while not under-estimating the difficulties faced by service users in changing their behaviour.

A sensitivity to, and an appreciation of, narrative webs

Narratives exist within a network, a web, of other stories: for example, my story about a difficult day at work is linked with the story of my line manager who provides supervision and my partner's story of having to live with a grump. The story of developing dementia is at once an individual story of illness, a couple's story of standing together and a professional story of diagnosis, prognosis, treatment and care. Narrative webs are made up of stories of individuals, stories of others, organisational stories and meta-stories (stories that seek to provide a framework for other stories – such as the historical meta-story of dementia as one of loss of ability and Self and decline until death). Such stories are not only linked but can be incorporated into each other – we tell stories about stories – and in so doing they are moulded, transformed, distorted, fragmented, repeated, enhanced, glossed over and so on.

An important aspect of such webs is that one can explore the web from any point. One can start, for example, from a story about attending a dementia cafe, which links with a story about cafes when on holiday, which links with stories about family members, which links with stories about weddings, and so on. All stories link, in some ways, to other stories.

The interactions between stories can thus be as important as the stories themselves because stories are, in a sense, performative; that is, by recounting a story we are expecting it to have an impact, to affect others and to affect other stories. These narrative relationships are thus imbued with not only intent (and all the emotional investment we might have placed in that) but also power.

Plummer (1994) writes of a sociology of stories in which some stories establish the agendas and rhetorics, are given privilege over other stories and act to close down the expression and even possibility of alternatives (see Chapter 1). On the other hand, some stories can open up new possibilities, empower and give voice to other stories, can resist, recuperate and recreate. An understanding of the nature of narrative power can help us understand the dynamics of narrative interaction and help us to focus on those stories that maintain the narrative web without pulling it out of shape. (For good examples of how stories can act to forward social justice, see Solinger et al, 2008.)

Another aspect of the web of narratives in which we find ourselves is the extent to which we allow others to contribute to our stories, to make a difference to our narrativised lives. Too often service users are seen as receivers (of care, services, compassion and so on) rather than active agents in a relationship, contributing as much as they receive. I would suggest that the very presence of the service user is a call, in the Levinasian sense of being confronted with a Face, to an ethical response, a response that creates us as humans. In other words, it is in responding to the Other that we become human (see Levinas, 1961).

The knack, of course, is to keep the web of stories in harmony. Over-emphasis on one story might distort the web by creating damaging tension between different stories. For example, in dementia, focusing on a story told through repeated psychometric testing of continuing decline in cognitive functioning can undermine other stories of retained abilities that uphold a sense of Self and self-esteem. An under-emphasis on a narrative of retained ability might weaken the threads between intersections. Keeping the balance is not necessarily easy.

Accumulation of narrative resources

If narratives can be woven into a web that supports the individual and those around her/him, then the extent of one's narrative resources determines the possible patterns and diversity of those webs. The more stories one has on which to draw, the more combinations are possible, the more links can be made. The wider the range of stories, the more intricate and detailed the web.

Having a stock of stories allows us to make sense of newly emerging stories by means of comparison to those we already know. Having a range of stories helps us to identify stories that might be missed if the range were narrower (see earlier regarding identifying narrative agency). This stock of stories, in order to support service users within a web of meaningful stories, needs to include stories of their past, present and future (see earlier regarding the establishment of an emerging plot), stories of those around them (family and friends), stories of strengths and abilities, of meaningful interactions and of how to go about navigating the journey on which they find themselves. In addition, on a wider scale, a stock of stories that includes stories that challenge the negative stereotypes surrounding service users, that celebrate aspects of life, that indicate possibilities rather than limitations, can help us resist the temptation to fit in with the current meta-narratives of welfare-ism, clienthood or moral inadequacy. While adversity may come to us all, how we approach it can depend on the narrative capital that we have accumulated over the years.

Further reflections

All ethical frameworks are open to criticism, and narrative ethics is no exception. While I have presented narrative ethics as a more caring alternative to principlism and more in line with social work values, it still does not prescribe any particular ethical route for practical action, a criticism that Clouser and Gert (1990) have levelled at principlism. This, Wilks (2005) notes, opens up narrative ethics to the criticism that it depends largely on individual application, situational vagaries and an open-ended responsibility to the Other, and is thus a relativistic approach to ethics unlike other frameworks that apply clearly defined moral principles (in contrast, see also Banks, 1998, for an argument in favour of ethics codes). However, it is these very conditions of narrative that promote personal accountability, a focus on the true needs of the Other/service user, and avoid doing violence to individual and cultural uniqueness. A narrative approach also focuses on the nature of the relationship between social worker and service user, allows for the constructive use of Self in that relationship and establishes a commitment to creating a mutually constituting narrative that affects both service user and social worker alike. I suggest that there is, currently, no other ethical framework that is able to do this.

In an explicitly moral sense, narrative ethics in social work practice opens up the possibility of 'see[ing] morality as a continual interpersonal task of becoming and remaining mutually intelligible. In this view, morality is something we all do together, in actual moral communities whose members express themselves and influence others by appealing to mutually recognized values and use those same values to refine understanding, extend consensus, and eliminate conflict' (Nelson, 2002, p 46).

Narrative ethics poses a means of not only examining service user stories for certain content – although that is one possibility – it offers a fundamental way of opening up and listening to the Other that necessitates a reaction grounded in the other person's best interests, not what we think those best interests should be. This means, in Nelson's words, 'it is time to tell the story forward' (2002, p 45) and to co-construct a new narrative that does justice to the many complex factors involved in a social worker/service user relationship while at the same time respecting their personal and professional needs. This will require creative ethical thinking and a great deal of personal responsibility, but this is part and parcel of ethical relationships in the first place.

5

Narrative and social policy

Of all the areas explored in this book, social policy is the one that most likely seems the least amenable to being understood as a narrative enterprise. After all, policy operates at a level of abstraction far from individual narratives or concerns and policy documents do not always have an obvious narrative structure. Nevertheless, I suggest that policy documents can be understood narratively – both as narrative constructions in themselves and as being embedded in, and drawing on, other narratives. This is important as social policy narratives form a major part of the environment in which social workers must operate, framing the possibilities for the development of legitimate social work narratives. In this chapter I explore some of the narrative features of social policy and examine one area of social policy in more detail.

Narrative policy analysis is also less well developed than narrative approaches to other areas. The literature on narrative policy analysis has remained, predominantly, within the confines of specialist publications, unlike, for example, issues around narrative and politics that find expression not only in academic and professional journals but also in popular media. Further, the rather limited literature is also somewhat abstruse, being written about technical debates concerning, for example, national budgeting systems (Roe, 1988) or the implementation of telephone number portability (Bridgman and Barry, 2002).

Consequently, my intent here is rather modest – to provide an outline of narrative policy analysis, its key uses and its strengths and weaknesses. Following this, I seek to apply such an analysis to the UK's National Dementia Strategy (NDS) and related documents as an illustration of method.

Definition

According to Roe (1994), narrative policy analysis is the application of contemporary literary theory to public policy issues, an application that aims to underscore the important and necessary role that narrative has in public policy. Understanding the stories behind and within public policy is therefore a means to understanding the background from which such policies emerge, the assumptions on which such policies are based and the trajectories that narrative establishes for the development and implementation of public policy.

The second aim of narrative policy analysis is to help reformulate what may seem intractable policy problems in ways that make them more responsive to conventional policy analytic approaches (Roe, 1994). Thus narrative is not in and of itself an analytical approach to policy but a means of facilitating policy analysis in more conventional ways.

Narrative policy analysis

In this approach to policy analysis there are a number of key features of narrative that need to be taken into account. First, stories that are used to describe and analyse policy issues must be understood as a force in themselves. Stories are not merely transporters of information but have an effect over and above the information that they convey. As indicated in Chapter 1, stories are inescapably rhetorical in that they seek to persuade the intended readership to accept the story as credible, reliable, truthful or believable. In order to understand policy narratives, therefore, we need to understand the intent behind them and the narrative and rhetorical elements they combine.

Second, policy narratives serve to underwrite and stabilise the assumptions for policy-making, and indeed decision-making more generally, in situations in which there are many unknowns, a high degree of interdependence and little, if any, agreement (Roe, 1994). In so doing, narrative can help manage uncertainty, establish internal coherence and clarify the positions of stakeholders. Further, the development of a meta-narrative – a narrative that can in some way encapsulate common ground and be open enough to allow for stakeholders to recognise how such a narrative will meet their interests and desires – can reduce conflict that may otherwise paralyse decision-making (see Hampton, 2011). This meta-narrative may also reframe controversies in ways that identify potential resolutions (Fischer, 2003), and van Eeten (2007) indicates how the meta-narrative does not have to provide a 'correct' version, merely one that allows a way forward and as such can be conducive to participatory decision-making.

Third, policy narratives are unlikely to change or modify even in the presence of contradicting empirical evidence. Just as with other narratives – for example, the narrative of child harm and dangerousness examined in Chapter 6 – policy narratives serve to provide a degree of certainty and coherence in the face of highly uncertain, complex and polarised situations. The trajectory established by the narrative both provides momentum to carry that narrative forward and helps to keep the policy or story on track when faced with challenges from alternative narratives.

Fourth, policy narratives, unlike the more decentred, non-linear narratives that we might find with regard to the self, tend to adhere to Aristotle's requirement that plots have beginnings, middles and ends. According to Kaplan (1993), policy narratives require this structure for pragmatic purposes; if one cannot identify a beginning to the story it is harder to argue the case that the current situation is as one describes it (for example, the existence of a culture of poverty) or to suggest actions that might help diminish the problem. A sense of ending is also desirable as an ending can bring together reports, studies and assessments that have no use except as part of a story that moves toward a more logical or happier ending.

In being framed within a linear structure, in managing uncertainty and complexity and in establishing a trajectory, policy narratives function to simplify situations (see Roe, 1991; Sutton, 1999). Such simplification may generate a narrative that motivates action, but it also runs the risk of falling foul of the fallacy of reduction – that is, reducing complex processes to simpler components or single causation, a fallacy ultimately unhelpful in understanding the situation (see Leach and Mearns, 1996).

Fifth, narrative policy analysis allows for consideration of competing voices in the process (Fischer, 2003), identifying and encouraging those voices and allowing them to be heard 'without prejudice or advantage' (Hampton, 2011, p 348); incorporating the issue of voice is intertwined with human rights and citizenship discussed in Chapter 2. Resultant policy narratives are thus polyphonic in that they articulate the stories of differing stakeholders. This is not to say that all voices are heard in the final policy narrative, as we shall see. Meta-narratives that seek the subscription of multifarious stakeholders cannot incorporate oppositional narratives – for example, a policy on mental health cannot include the narrative of the medical model of mental illness and the narrative of the conspiracy model, that is, that mental illness is a myth. Identifying excluded voices is thus important in analysing policy from a narrative perspective.

Sixth, narratives, like metaphors, have the ability to bring together what at first seems distant into something close – in other words, to link the abstract with the personal. With the framing of a problematic situation within a narrative the reader may be better able to 'comprehend or grasp as a whole the chain of meanings in one act of synthesis' (Ricoeur, 1976, p 72, cited in Kaplan, 1993, p 172). In this, as indicated in our discussion of framing in Chapter 1, such narratives can help people understand novel situations by reference to categories and other narratives with which they are already familiar.

Further, collective narratives realised in social policy create both the space within which individuals exercise their citizenship rights – their rights to be heard – and formal representations of identity — for example, what constitutes the formal representation of an ageing identity (see Powell and Edwards, 2002). In so doing, policy narratives define the space in which individual identities can be legitimately performed (Powell and Edwards, 2002). These definitions and spaces may, of course, not be the ones that the individuals so defined and bounded would choose for themselves, but policy narratives clearly link the personal with social norms, perceptions and interests (for examples of links between personal and policy narratives, see Mullan, 1999; McDonough, 2001; Sharf, 2001).

Finally, critiques of policy narratives may serve to increase uncertainty and undermine the assumptions of the decision-making process, leaving the decision-makers without the means to make the transition from the narrative that is being critiqued to a new narrative that might justifiably replace it. As critique does not necessarily have its own story but could simply be point-by-point objections to elements of the narrative, critique can raise but not answer doubts. For the policy-making process to survive, therefore, it requires a new, better story to replace the one discredited by critique.

While narrative policy analysis seems to have many advantages in terms of drawing out the implications of policy issues, of linking the personal and the abstract, reconciling the stances of different stakeholders and communication of policy in understandable terms and form, there are two aspects that need to be held in mind. The first is the issue of voice. We saw in Chapter 2 that narrative voice is linked to the notion of human rights and that individuals and groups can be narratively dispossessed in a number of ways that silence or negate their voice. It is the same in the policy-making process. In narrative policy decision-making the construction of the meta-narrative is the work of the policy analyst(s), not the direct making of those involved. As such the approach may fail to fully capture the richness and nuances of the debate and competing positions and in particular the dialogical nature of debate that can produce creative insights that more univocal approaches may not. In other words, narrative policy-making is undertaken at least at one remove from the voices of those involved.

A narrative analysis of the National Dementia Strategy

In 2009 the UK government published the National Dementia Strategy (NDS) (DH, 2009a). This followed extensive consultation with 50 consultation events attended by approximately 4,000 individuals and approximately 600 written responses to the draft strategy (DH, 2009b). The NDS was generally applauded as a major move forward in taking seriously the issue of dementia through the promotion of awareness and understanding, early diagnosis and support and living well with dementia, although there were reservations about how well the strategy might be implemented, and the government was criticised for not making enough extra funds available for research into dementia (see Boseley, 2009). Indeed, the reservations about the strategy were not about the contents, style, assumptions or intent, but concerned the commitment of the government to its implementation.

The NDS is, essentially, a rhetorical document, aimed at persuading particular stakeholders and the general public to accept the direction proposed by the strategy and, where appropriate, to take action to implement the strategy. As a rhetorical text it seeks to be clear about its central action (Bennett and Feldman, 1981) – that of addressing three key areas of concern regarding dementia: awareness and understanding, early diagnosis and support and living well with dementia. It develops a trajectory for its preferred plot and sub-plots and populates these with a range of characters, each with specific roles, with these being framed so as to align with other policy narratives. The strategy is polyphonous in incorporating the voices of diverse stakeholders but more univocal (monophonous) in its view of dementia. I suggest that the polyphony is limited to those voices that share the singular perception of dementia espoused in the report.

The NDS is not written as a narrative, but it contains many of the features of one. Appearing as a statement of commitment to a particular course of action it embeds the narrative notion of movement from one position, disrupted by a complicating action (or actions), to another position – that is, it is emplotted.

The originary position is one in which healthy adults face:

… progressive decline in multiple areas of function, including decline in memory, reasoning, communication skills and the ability to carry out daily activities. Alongside this decline, individuals may develop behavioural and psychological symptoms such as depression, psychosis, aggression and wandering, which cause problems in themselves, which complicate care, and which can occur at any stage of the illness. (DH, 2009a, p 15)

This is set against a backdrop of approximately 700,000 people with dementia, costing the nation about £17 billion a year and within a projected trajectory of the number of people with dementia rising to 1.4 million and a cost of over £50 billion per year in the next 30 years.

It is recognised that there is, currently, no cure for dementia and thus, if the UK is to avoid the 'devastating impact' of dementia, action needs to be taken with this action setting a different trajectory, that of 'living well with dementia' (the title of the NDS).

We therefore have an originary position of people who are threatened by dementia with action being taken to establish a second position, that of living well despite the dementia, that is, a plot. I would also suggest that there are a number of sub-plots to be found in the NDS. One of these is the government's desire to be seen as raising the status of the UK vis-à-vis other European countries:

> International comparisons suggest that the UK is in the bottom third of European performance in terms of diagnosis and treatment, with less than half the activity of France, Sweden, Ireland and Spain. (DH, 2009a, p 17)

I suggest this because the international comparison is actually irrelevant to the main plot line of addressing the potential impact of dementia. Dementia is, in this plot, set to rise, and with it costs, regardless of how the UK compares with other countries. The insertion of this secondary complicating action serves to tie in the strategy with other narratives of the UK's standing in the international community.

The main plot of the NDS can also be understood in formalist terms (see Chapter 1). The people, threatened by a villain or dragon (that is, dementia), are to be protected by the King (government) who despatches the hero (in the NDS, a number of people and stakeholders) on a quest (that is, to develop 'health and social services for dementia that are fit for the 21st century', Alan Johnson, quoted in DH, 2009a, p 3). Those charged with the quest, health and social care professionals in the main, face a number of challenges – lack of awareness and understanding, late diagnosis and lack of good quality services – which must be overcome if they are to reach the goal 'for people with dementia and their family carers to be helped to live well with dementia, no matter what the stage of their illness or where they are in the health and social care system' (DH, 2009a, p 21). They will be helped by a public information campaign, commissioning of services, training, organisational changes, other policy commitments and an evidence base for practice.

Here we have all the elements of a folktale in modern form – the villain, the hero, the despatcher, the helper, the hinderer, a quest (see Propp, 1968). I have used the term 'quest' quite deliberately as it has a dual function here. The first is, simply, to capture the plot of the NDS in narrative terms. The second reason to use the term is that the plot of the NDS appears as an example of a quest narrative in Frank's (1995) sense of the term. Arthur Frank, in his discussion of illness narratives, identifies three primary forms: the restitution narrative, the chaos narrative and the quest narrative.

The restitution narrative is, it seems, the preferred one, certainly in Western modern society. This narrative takes the form of 'Yesterday I was well, today I am ill, tomorrow I will be well again.' There is a belief here, deeply embedded in modern medicine, that health is, can and should be restorable. We see this in Talcott Parson's exploration of the sick role (1951) where those who are sick are expected to try to get well, to seek competent medical help and to cooperate with medical care to get well. Conversely, behaviours that induce or maintain sickness are themselves seen as deviant or even signs of illness – for example, non-compliance with treatment or Munchausen syndrome, where an individual induces or fabricates illness, both of which appear as categories in the *Diagnostic and statistical manual-IV-TR.*

The restitution narrative, however, does not work very well for chronic illness or disability in that it is unlikely that previous good health can ever be restored. In terms of dementia, in the NDS the restitution narrative is dismissed from the outset: dementia is progressive (DH, 2009a, p 10) and terminal (p 10) and, barring a medical breakthrough (p 5), we have to deal with it in the best way that we can.

The chaos narrative expresses the fear of being overwhelmed by the illness. Underlying this form of illness narrative is the message that things are not going to get better. Human frailty and vulnerability are revealed as potentially applicable to all – which provokes anxiety. The NDS can be read as an attempt to counter, or at least avoid, slipping into a chaos narrative. In the absence of a cure there has been a sense of therapeutic nihilism around dementia (Cheston and Bender, 1999), that is, a sense that nothing can be done. Indeed, the NDS, directly states that there:

> ... is a marked reluctance on the part of primary care to be directly involved in the diagnosis of dementia for reasons that include: *the belief that nothing can be done for dementia*; risk avoidance; concerns about competency; and concerns about the availability of resources. (DH, 2009a, p 36; emphasis added)

In contrast, the NDS seeks to promote an alternative story – that while there is no cure, there is still a lot that can be done, and that people with dementia and their carers can still live well:

> ... it is also clear that there is a vast amount that can be done to
> improve and maintain quality of life in dementia. Positive input from
> health and social care services and from the third sector and carers
> of people with dementia can make all the difference between living
> well with dementia and having a poor quality of life. (Bannerjee and
> Owen, quoted in DH, 2009a, p 7)

For the authors of the NDS, a chaos narrative is not acceptable.

The quest story is one in which the person accepts that s/he may not get better and seeks alternative ways of being ill, and sees illness in a different light. This is what the NDS strives to do – the quest for 'living well with dementia': 'Dementia is not an immediate death sentence; there is life to be lived with dementia and it can be of good quality' (DH, 2009, p 29).

The importance of plot in the NDS is that it provides, as Kaplan (1993) has suggested, a justification for the actions incorporated within the policy. Without a hopeful plot, moving toward 'living well', there is little reason to engage with any of the policy objectives.

Motivation to action is also promoted through the simplification of the situation so as to limit ambiguity and uncertainty (see Roe, 1991; Sutton, 1999). In narrative terms this concerns the clarity of the central action or cause (see Bennett and Feldman, 1981). We see this process of simplification in the NDS in a number of ways. First, in how dementia is viewed as a syndrome, a medical disorder rather than a natural part of ageing. This might seem a reasonable enough perspective but it is a simplified one. In taking this perspective the authors of the NDS are ruling out other explanations or perspectives on dementia, presuming that the one being presented is the correct one. Anthropologically, for example, it can be demonstrated that dementia, the predominant feature of which is memory loss, is a peculiarly Western conceptualisation linked to the West's focus on an individualistic, essentialist Self (see Hashmi, 2009, and Chapter 1, this book). In other cultures, China, for example, memory loss is seen as a normal part of ageing and does not undermine a person's status in a society in which longevity is associated with high value (see Ikels, 2002). Lest such a view be thought of as peculiarly oriental, dementia is seen among many people as part of the ageing process. Research undertaken by Alzheimer's Australia Vic (2008) indicated that nine of the twelve minority ethnic groups surveyed thought dementia to be entirely or in part due to the natural process of ageing.

The privileging of the medical narrative of dementia is not as obvious a choice as it first might appear. This narrative itself has a history, and while it is the predominant narrative, it is not the only possible one. Lyman (1989) and Bond (1992) both challenge the bio-medicalisation of dementia, and Kitwood argued that there was little evidence of a direct relationship between the symptoms of dementia and damage to specific parts of the brain, and only a moderate correlation between the severity of dementia and overall brain pathology (see Kitwood, 1996), thus challenging the empirical basis for the medial narrative. Kitwood further argued that dementia might be related to psychobiography and capitalism (see Kitwood, 1990), a position that may gain some support from Ineichen (1996) in his discussion of possible explanations for the increase in the prevalence of dementia in China.

More recently, Whitehouse (2008) has argued strongly against the scientification of Alzheimer's, saying that this is a partial and ultimately misguided approach to brain ageing. For Whitehouse, the medical narrative is but one possibility, and:

> The story of brain aging is ultimately your own story to tell, not mine, not your doctor's, and certainly not the self-interested pharmaceutical companies or research institutions that capitalize on our biological classification of AD [Alzheimer's disease] as a disease. (Whitehouse, 2008, p 43)

The problem with the simplification involved in the NDS approach is that alternative narratives are, by necessity, seen as wrong (referred to more kindly in the NDS as 'misunderstandings'), and those who tell such stories are in need of education to raise their awareness. However, if everyone were to tell their own story of brain ageing, there would be little basis for promoting one policy over another.

This brings us on to the presence of polyphony in the NDS. In this respect the NDS is conflicted. On the one hand, it clearly states that many voices have been listened to in the consultation process and indeed, the list of contributors is impressive (see DH, 2009b, Appendix 1[a] and [b]). On the other hand, it would appear from the consultation that everyone is in accord with the assumptions made in the NDS and the medicalised model, when, if one explores the wider literature, accord is far less than universal. We do not know to what extent such competing voices were raised in the consultation process, but certainly voices contradicting the central premise(s) of the NDS found no expression in the final document. As such the NDS may be seen as an example of Plummer's points about how 'expert' (in the case of the NDS, medical) stories might be privileged while lay ones marginalised and excluded, how access to stories is prevented or facilitated and how some stories degrade, control and dominate others (Plummer, 1994; see also Chapter 1).

The polyphonic nature of the NDS also serves a rhetorical function in that it presents the NDS as being a response by the government to a process of consultation and thus being aligned with the democratic process. Numerous times in the NDS certain stakeholders, most notably carers and people living with dementia, are referred to as being fully involved and shaping the plan. The list of contributing organisations includes local authorities, voluntary and community sector agencies, health authorities and medical organisations, at least one pharmaceutical company and various pharmaceutical groups. Constructing the NDS on the basis of this consultation allows for these stakeholders to identify how their interests will be met by signing up to the policy and thus they can engage in decisions concerning its implementation (see Hampton, 2011).

The NDS is not only polyphonous but also heteroglossic in that it embeds a series of social meanings and ideologies into its framework. The first set of meanings concerns the nature of dementia as a syndrome, a phenomenon to be understood, framed and addressed in medical terms. This approach to dementia is illustrative of the process of medicalisation more generally (see Furedi, 2006, and Conrad, 2007, for a discussion of the medicalisation thesis). We touched on this earlier when we discussed the exclusion of alternative narratives. The second set of meanings embedded in the NDS surrounds cultural issues of loss, especially the loss of cognitive ability. Post (2000) terms this elevation of cognitive ability 'hypercognition' and it is little wonder in a hypercognitive society that the fear of forgetting is so strong that more people over the age of 65 fear developing dementia (39 per cent) than developing cancer, heart disease and stroke (Alzheimer's Society, 2008). In Chapter 3 I discussed the essentialist Self, 'a bounded, unique, more or less integrated motivational and cognitive universe; a dynamic center of awareness, emotion, judgment, and action organized into a distinctive whole' (Geertz, 1974, p 31), and it is this sense of Self that lies behind the idea of dementia as the loss of the Self. With the onset and progression of dementia, the integrated cognitive universe starts to fragment and with this fragmentation awareness, emotion and judgement start to fluctuate and erode.

Policy narratives, like all narratives, exist in an environment populated by other narratives. On the one hand, as indicated earlier, a narrative might set itself up in opposition to other narratives; on the other, it might draw on narratives that support its premises, preferred plot or characterisations. In some cases the narratives which are drawn on have to be inferred as they leave only traces – for example, the essentialist Self that underlies much of person-centred care (see Chapter 3). In other cases, such as the NDS, the narrative environment is made explicit. Annex 2 of the NDS discusses the context of the strategy, listing eight reports and policy initiatives that are directly relevant to dementia and three wider policy documents that have an impact on the strategy. Thus the NDS was written within a network of policy narratives that helped shaped what could be, and what was said, in the strategy, and served to exclude other, highly relevant factors. Let me take just one example.

In 2008, the government issued *Carers at the heart of 21st-century families and communities* (DH, 2008), an update to the Carers' Strategy of 1999. In this document the government laid out its intentions and plans to support family carers, stating that 'a key advantage to the provision of care by a family member, friend or partner is that such an approach can result in personalised, responsive, expert and high-quality care that is in the best interests of the person being supported' (DH, 2008, p 40). The NDS picks up this theme when it states that family carers are 'the most valuable resource for people with dementia' (DH, 2009a, p 49). The government also acknowledges the personal and financial costs that are oft-times involved in the caring role, and the NDS proposes a range of means to alleviate these burdens. Further, in 2009 it was estimated that informal carers of people living with dementia saved the government approximately £6 billion a year. It is not surprising, then, that family carers are cast in the role of heroes.

Having developed this policy narrative about family carers other possible narratives are excluded, even though from the outside they may seem highly relevant. The NDS carries one paragraph on the possibility of abuse – on page 49 – where it says, 'People with dementia are known to be an "at risk" group in terms of abuse, particularly (although not exclusively) through financial exploitation, fraud and theft. Reliance on others for support to manage finances can expose people with dementia to the risk of abuse.' What is interesting about this paragraph is that it does not say who might be the abusers. Research suggests that approximately one third of family carers admit to significant levels of abusive behaviour toward their relative and over half to some abusive behaviour (Cooper et al, 2009), although the figures may, of course, be higher given an understandable reluctance to admit to such behaviour. This view of family carers as potential abusers does not fit easily with the general respect that family carers are granted, and I would therefore suggest, cannot find a voice in the NDS. To allow such a voice to be heard would contradict previous policy narratives and also undermine the NDS itself. In other words, the NDS is shaped not only by the consultation process but an underlying ideology to which the government is committed through previous policy narratives.

Further reflections

In this chapter I have tried to illustrate how one might analyse policy documents through a narrative lens. Policy narratives are, essentially, rhetorical in that they seek to mobilise support for the proposed actions, and to this end such narratives navigate between the need for legitimacy derived from wide consultation and the simplification necessary to justify and clarify the central action of the plot trajectory established in the policy. Policy can thus be seen as negotiating the constant tension between inclusion and exclusion of multiple narratives. The NDS negotiated this process by declaring its polyphony through its list of contributors while remaining silent about possible alternative narratives about dementia itself and also about points of focus of the policy, for example, family carers. In so doing the NDS opened up space for stories to be told about certain aspects of dementia and closed down opportunities for other stories. In the light of the NDS it would be difficult, for example, to mobilise action for the view that dementia is part of the natural process of ageing. The NDS does, however, manage very effectively to link personal and policy narratives, at least for those who sign up to the strategy.

Part 3
Application

6

Plot, characterisation and rhetoric in child protection

Having discussed the relevance and uses of narrative in respect of social work concerns of values, Self, policy and ethics, we now turn to how narrative can be used to cast new understandings of social work practice. In this chapter we apply narrative theory to the area of child protection, looking in particular at plot, trajectory, characterisation and rhetoric, using a single case of alleged child abuse, details of which appear elsewhere (see Baldwin, 2008a). In Chapter 7 we look at how the Self is constituted within the discourse of mental illness, and how we might draw on other narratives about mental illness or madness to inform social work practice. In Chapter 8 we turn our attention to meta-narratives as they have shaped disability discourse over time. Such an approach to social work texts is limited but not unknown. Hall (1997) argues convincingly for a narrative analysis of social work, and Hyden (1997) employs an explicitly literary framework in his analysis of texts in child protection in Sweden. Here I extend this work by focusing in detail on one particular case, a case of alleged Munchausen syndrome by proxy (MSbP), as an illustrative example of how these narrative features are at play in the investigation and prosecution of a case of alleged child abuse. The lessons that can be drawn from this case are in many ways transferable not only to other situations and alleged forms of abuse but to other fields of social work as well.

Background

The mother, 'P', was a US citizen living in the UK. Following an acrimonious divorce in the US her ex-husband made numerous attempts to gain custody of their son, on his fourth attempt making allegations of MSbP abuse. No such concerns were raised prior to this fourth attempt and the ex-husband made no indications that there were any child protection concerns whatsoever prior to this. P was later charged with a felony offence of child abuse of MSbP based on the administration of laxatives (poisoning), but the jury substantially rejected the District Attorney's argument and found P guilty only of a misdemeanour and, according to later proceedings in the Juvenile Court, there had been no findings of MSbP in the criminal case.

P became pregnant and social services, following receipt of information and cursory preliminary investigation, removed the child, 'S', shortly after birth and placed her with foster parents. There then followed further investigations and extensive court proceedings in which the local authority sought to free the child for adoption on the grounds that she was at risk from P. At first the local authority argued for estoppel – they tried to argue that the court in the US had already decided the facts of the case and thus the UK court need only concern itself with what action was required to protect the child. This argument was rejected by the court and full proceedings commenced.

During the final hearing the local authority argued, on the basis of reports by a UK expert, that P had attempted to harm her child, S, during the pregnancy through giving a history of symptoms such that steroids were administered unnecessarily and delaying admission to hospital against medical advice. The judge rejected each and every argument that the mother had attempted to harm S and the argument that the mother had displayed abnormal health-seeking behaviour on her own account while in the UK. Faced with this rejection, the local authority, unwilling to give up the case, were then forced to argue a far weaker and more subjectively evaluated case based on dangerousness – that the mother had harmed her son in the US and was thus a danger to her daughter in the UK, even though she had done nothing to suggest that she had or would harm her daughter. Following extensive hearings in which P was forced to represent herself because her legal counsel abandoned her at the beginning of the final hearing and the judge refused a short adjournment for P to seek other legal counsel, the judge ruled that the mother had harmed her son in the US, posed a danger to her daughter and that the child should be freed for adoption. When P asked for leave to appeal the judge refused, also denying her full access to the transcripts of the case, thus hindering her in applying for leave to appeal. The parents then applied to the Court of Appeal but leave to appeal was refused, with the two justices holding to the view that Justice Wall 'was throughout meticulous in ensuring fairness, and scrupulously careful to consider any points that went to the advantage of the mother…'. An application to the European Court of Human Rights (ECHR) followed, and the local authority was informed and asked not to proceed with the adoption until the outcome was known. The authority ignored the request and proceeded with the adoption. The argument before the ECHR was heard in public in March 2002. The government reiterated the position taken by the local authority in the domestic proceedings that P represented a danger to the child, S, and that the actions of the local authority were justified in order to protect the child. Furthermore, they argued that the domestic hearings were fair because, despite being unrepresented, P, as Justice Wall had stated, had a good knowledge of the documents, had been legally represented up until the final hearing and all parties (the local authority, the guardian ad litem and their legal teams) were of the opinion that it was a fair hearing. In July 2002 the ECHR ruled that:

- the original hearings had violated Article 6 of the Human Rights Act (the right to a fair hearing) and 'not only gave the appearance of unfairness but prevented the applicants from putting forward their case in a proper and effective manner';
- given the 'serious disadvantage' to the parents by not being legally represented, it could not 'be excluded that this might have had an effect on the decisions reached and eventual outcome for the family as a whole';

- the 'draconian step of removing S from her mother shortly after birth was not supported by relevant and sufficient reasons and [...] cannot be regarded as having been necessary in a democratic society for the purpose of safeguarding S' (*P, C & S vs The United Kingdom ECHR* [2002] Application no 56547/00).

The UK government was ordered to pay damages and costs, but because the adoption had been completed peremptorily without waiting for the outcome of the European hearing, the child remains permanently removed from her birth family. (For further details of the case see Baldwin, 2005, 2008a.)

Emplotment

Emplotment, according to Ricoeur (1985), is the organisation of temporally successive events, scenes and descriptions in order to construct causal continuity. In other words, plot is not simply the recounting of events but the structuring of these events in a particular way for particular purposes. When we examine the plot of P, C & S we see that from the outset social services were viewing this as a case of MSbP. Without reviewing the US case for themselves and relying only on the perspective of those who had prosecuted the case in the US, social services applied for estoppel – they claimed that the case had already been heard and decided on in the US, and all that was required in the UK was a decision about the disposal of the case, what should happen to the index child, S. On several occasions social services attempted this argument and at each point it was refused. Indeed, it is quite clear from the US transcripts that the judge in the criminal trial made no findings of MSbP and the Juvenile Court documents explicitly state that there were no such findings. Social services were then placed in the position of having to emplot the UK case as one of MSbP for themselves if they were to remain in line with their previous commitment. They did this in a number of ways.

First, they started to enrol other professionals to support their narrative of MSbP. In doing this they sought an expert psychiatric evaluation. When this came back in favour of working with the family, social services hid the report from the parents and the courts and sought a second evaluation, which was more critical of the parents and advocated adoption (a recommendation in line with the emerging plot). In addition, they sought out further details from the US, but only from those involved in prosecuting the case against the mother. Going even further, they attempted to influence the mother's own independent psychiatric expert by approaching him with the issues and questions that they wanted answered – an approach both inappropriate and against proper practice. In enrolling others, social services set the parameters within which narratives could be told, that is, that any story had to be told within the frame of MSbP.

A second way of establishing emplotment was to interpret the mother's behaviour (and, indeed, the behaviour of the father and other family members) as supporting the narrative of MSbP or justifying social services' decisions. So, for example, when the mother refused to comply with the demands made on her by social services she was seen as hostile – a trait that served the emerging plot of the need to put the child forward for adoption. The paediatrician, an expert in MSbP, interpreted many of the medical records (not ever seeing the mother or the child) as indicating MSbP behaviour – for example, he saw no need for steroid injections during pregnancy so interpreted these as the result of the mother providing misleading or deceitful medical history. (The judge rejected this, along with many other such interpretations.)

Third, the social worker reported at least two incidents that fitted with the MSbP narrative but that were essentially untrue. The first was a report that the mother, having refused medical advice to remain in hospital, had returned home and then later had to be rushed to hospital in an ambulance, thus causing a delay to her Caesarean section. This incident was pure fabrication. The neonatologist confirmed that the mother had not acted on his advice by going home and that the delay in the operation was due to the hospital, not the mother. The ambulance service received no emergency call and the mother arrived at the hospital in her car, driven by her husband. However, stories of drama, thwarting medical advice and endangering a child are stock in trade stories in cases of MSbP and it is reasonable to see this particular story as helping to reinforce the argument that this was a case of MSbP.

The second incident, while not fabricated, was a result of extremely poor investigation by the social worker involved. She heard from somewhere that the mother had reported a house fire while in the US. Without checking any of the facts with the mother, the social worker contacted the fire department about an address at which the mother had previously lived. The fire department reported that there had been no fire at that address but at one nearby. The social worker then reported this incident as a further example of the mother lying about dramatic events. Had the social worker checked with the mother, she would have known that the fire was actually in a storage unit in a different US state and the mother could have provided her with photographs and the fire report. It is important to remember, however, that in the MSbP literature, false reports of house fires are viewed as indicative of further MSbP behaviour, and so this story was again in line with the narrative that social services wished to develop.

Trajectory

Once established, a plot can be understood to have a trajectory – a direction, impetus and an end goal – and once in motion, it can be kept on course using a number of narrative techniques. Indeed, Hyden (1997) suggests that it is the purpose of the narrative to justify the conclusion of the narrative:

> The plot of both the social reports and the psychiatric commitment reports could be described as the "logic" which inevitably forces the narrative characters into a situation where only one option seems viable: the proposed institutional action. This end is the starting point

and gives all actions prior to this point their significance. (Hyden, 1997, p 253; original emphasis)

The trajectory is thus the progression toward the only viable option, and therefore factors that might deflect that trajectory need to be dealt with if the plot is to be kept on track. Three processes can be identified as part of this trajectory work: the reconfiguration of supporting characters, narrative smoothing and the protection of preferred narrators.

The first of these, the reconfiguration of supporting characters, can be seen at play on a number of occasions during the investigations and proceedings. When one configuration was threatened or a supporting actor seen as a weak link, the configuration shifted so as to keep the trajectory on course. For example, in their initial court applications social services relied heavily on the evidence of the paediatrician involved in the US proceedings. Initially, the judge in the UK proceedings, Justice Wall, stated unequivocally that this paediatrician's presence was required but the paediatrician refused to testify, and in a volte face, Justice Wall then ruled that the paediatrician need not testify and a UK paediatrician/expert in MSbP was engaged to evaluate the US medical records. This reconfiguration can be seen to have performed an important function in maintaining the trajectory in that it removed the opportunity for P to cross-examine a key witness as to the discrepancies, inaccuracies, inconsistencies and contradictions in the US paediatrician's various reports and the veracity and reliability of the US paediatrician's evidence was removed from the debate (having simply been assumed by the UK paediatrician).

A second process in maintaining the trajectory is what Spence (1986) calls narrative smoothing. This is the process whereby the narrative line is unified to create thematic consistency and purpose that serve to maintain the trajectory of a narrative by minimising or eliminating potential disruptions.

Narrative smoothing can be seen at work in the case of P, C & S in the use of patterning and recuperation (see Baldwin, 2000) to deflect counter-arguments. For example, the UK paediatrician claimed that the medical records indicated a pattern of presentations that indicated MSbP abuse. Challenged by the mother's argument that on many occasions the medical records showed that something was wrong, the UK paediatrician replied that it was not individual presentations that were important but the overall pattern (patterning). In other words, the trajectory of MSbP could not be disrupted by pointing out evidence to the contrary. In response, P submitted a detailed rebuttal of the paediatrician's interpretation of the US medical records (detailing symptoms, tests, results and treatments and numerous inaccuracies in his report). The UK paediatrician made no attempt to counter these challenges but recuperated P's action as being 'typical of a Munchausen mother'. In other words, P's attempt to defend herself by challenging the medical records and interpretation of these was indicative of MSbP behaviour. The MSbP trajectory was thus maintained through the processes of patterning and recuperation.

A second process in maintaining the trajectory was the protection of preferred narrators. Although Family Court proceedings are supposedly impartial, it is possible to detect biases in the protection of certain narrators from the consequences of their failings. So, for example, the guardian ad litem was silent as to the fabrications in the social worker's report (see earlier), thus glossing over failings in the local authority's narrative and the credibility of their prime narrator. Similarly, Justice Wall prevented the mother cross-examining certain witnesses as to their supposed expertise and track record, thus protecting their testimony being questioned on these grounds. But such protection went further in that both the UK paediatrician and UK psychiatrist were protected against the potential consequences of their failing as the psychiatrist's evidence was accepted despite his having lost both copies of his original notes (so no challenge as to the accuracy of these could be raised), and the UK paediatrician's interpretation of the US medical records was accepted uncritically, even though he was not an expert in the field of gastroenterology, under which the illnesses of the US child fell. These two factors could have been interpreted as incompetence and stepping outside of expertise, but were not. This bias in treatment of narrators can be seen by contrasting the treatment of the mother whose evidentiary failings were allowed to be probed in detail so as to cast doubt on her credibility and reliability.

Characterisation

If we now turn to characterisation we can see how social services sought to characterise the mother in line with the archetypal mother in the MSbP literature.

In the literature on the sociology of health and illness, there is the concept of character work. This work seeks to uncover the moral essence of the person by presenting their behaviour, thoughts and feelings in a particular fashion. Strong (1979) reports character work being rarely used by the subjects of his research, but it seems that such characterisation is fundamental to cases of MSbP. Schreier and Libow (1993) view 'lying as the essential mode of interaction' among MSbP mothers, representing 'a particular form of "character perversion"' (p 85) and integrated into characterlogic traits (p 95).

There is no doubt that social services characterised the mother in line with the MSbP archetypal mother. She was frequently portrayed as deceitful, untrustworthy, hostile, non-compliant and obstructive, manipulative, medically knowledgeable, unable to establish stable relationships or to maintain stable employment, and potentially dangerous. Some of these claims were simply unsubstantiated – for example, despite claiming that the mother had previously engaged in threatening behaviour and had restraining orders taken out against her, social services were unable to produce any evidence for this. Other claims relied on interpreting the mother's actions through the lens of MSbP when other explanations were available and, perhaps, more appropriate. For example, the paediatrician on whose reports social services were relying to support their narrative of MSbP, stated that, 'It is customary in these cases [that is, cases of MSbP] for the alleged perpetrator or their legal representative to break down the alleged abuse into its component parts and attempt to "shout down" the evidence piece by piece. This is illustrated here' and 'It is customary for the parent or their legal representative to attempt to limit the analysis of the medical history to the index child only.... This is illustrated here.' In doing so, the paediatrician located the mother's actions in defending herself within the discourse of MSbP.

The full effect of characterisation can be illustrated by comparing what stands as due process under the law with the paediatrician's claims. Twining, in discussing the rationalist model of adjudication, states that:

> The direct end of adjective law is rectitude of decision through correct application of valid substantive laws ... and through accurate determination of the true past facts material to precisely specified allegations expressed in categories defined in advance by law (ie facts in issue) proved to specified standards of probability or likelihood on the basis of the careful and rational weighing of evidence which is both relevant and reliable, presented in a form designed to bring out the truth and discover untruth, to supposedly competent and impartial decision makers, with adequate safeguards against corruption and mistake and adequate provision for review and appeal. (Twining, 1990, pp 72-3)

In this context the mother's arguments can be seen as perfectly legitimate – by questioning individual events (the evidence) she could be seen as attempting to 'accurately determine true past facts', for, if indeed the child in the US was ill on the occasions under discussion, the 'pattern' so frequently referred to by the paediatrician would break down. She could also be seen as addressing 'precisely specified allegations', that is, the allegations of administration of laxatives on identifiable occasions, and contributing to the 'careful and rational weighing' of 'relevant and reliable' evidence (for example, by ensuring proper examination of the documentary evidence and by focusing on the index child).

Within this legal framework, the arguments presented by the mother appear in a far more positive light than when framed within that of MSbP. My argument here is therefore not about the merits of the mother's arguments but about the framing of these within one discourse rather than another. The choice of context is thus part of character work in that it impugns the mother by association with the nebulous and unsubstantiated 'customary' behaviour of MSbP mothers and thus undermines her credibility by 'poisoning the well', 'a tactic to silence an opponent violating her right to put forward arguments on an issue' (Walton, 2006, p 273).

In contrast to the portrayal of the mother, others are rendered in very favourable lights. I have explored in detail elsewhere (Baldwin, 2011) how the paediatrician sought to establish his authorial credibility through presenting himself in a certain way – careful, methodical, qualified and experienced and so on – glossing over potential difficult areas or features that might be questioned (for example, lack of expertise in gastroenterology and toxicology) and inviting the reader to join with him in viewing this as a case of MSbP. Indeed, the paediatrician was viewed in such a way that the judge, even after dismissing much of the paediatrician's report as being wrong, still felt able to say essentially that the paediatrician had tried to find in favour of the mother but had been forced to concede to the weight of the evidence. Similarly, even though social services had hidden a key report from the parents and the courts, a report that could have had a major impact on the case as their chosen expert had said that she was willing to be involved in working with the family, Justice Wall merely criticised social services for a lack of judgement in providing the parents a stick with which they might beat social services, rather than viewing the actions of social services as unfair, distorting due process, deceitful and unprofessional. In effect, in so doing, the judge turned professionally and legally dubious actions on the part of social services against the parents – implying that the parents were acting unreasonably by wanting to call social services to account for their actions.

We therefore see a variety of characterisations and methods of characterisation at play in this case. On the one hand, the mother is subjected both to direct and explicit and indirect and implied negative characterisation while the paediatrician is allowed, without question, to present himself directly in positive terms, defended against cross-examination on these matters and protected from criticism even when substantially wrong in his interpretation and testimony. At the same time, social services is implicitly characterised as reliable and professional by turning evidence to the contrary to imply unreasonableness on the part of the parents.

Rhetoric

While I have indicated a few rhetorical features of the case in the earlier discussion of characterisation, I now turn to a brief discussion of rhetoric (see also Chapter 1) in action in the argument that was made by social services, based on the paediatrician's reports. This aspect of rhetoric is what Aristotle terms 'logos' and is, perhaps, more subtle and less immediately obvious than both ethos and pathos. Here I focus on one particular element of the argument – that of the implicit syllogism in the narrative of alleged guilt and dangerousness.

Syllogistic reasoning takes the form of two statements that lead necessarily to a conclusion, and can be illustrated in the following way:

> All men are mortal
> Socrates is a man.
> Therefore Socrates is mortal.

In such reasoning, nothing new is added in the final statement, it being merely the logical outcome of the first two. Such reasoning is based on certain assumptions (in the above case, a non-contentious one): that all men are mortal and that Socrates falls into the category indicated by the term 'men'. To be certain of a true outcome, the premises of the arguments (the first two statements) need to be true. If either were false, or at least contestable, then the conclusion would not be logically certain, as in the following example:

> All conscientious objectors are cowards.
> Bert Brocklesby was a conscientious objector.
> Therefore Bert Brocklesby was a coward.

In this argument, the first premise is at best arguable and at worst plain wrong, and the second seems to be true and therefore the conclusion cannot follow, with any certainty, from the premises (and indeed seems completely wrong in the light of his convictions and actions which indicate a high degree of bravery – see Rennell, 2008).

Although not expressed in such formal syllogistic a fashion, the narrative constructed by social services was based on the following syllogism:

> In cases of MSbP a pattern of presentation and behaviour can be identified.
> In this case the same pattern of presentation and behaviour can be identified.
> Therefore this is a case of MSbP.

Expressed in such a way, the premises are transparent and questions can easily be asked about how we know whether either of the premises is valid. For example, authors such as Mart (2002) have demonstrated the statistical and logical flaws and difficulties regarding the supposed indicators of MSbP and the MSbP profile, thus questioning the truth or reliability of the first premise. The second premise is resolved empirically – are the pattern and behaviours found in this case? I have illustrated earlier how certain behaviours were framed by MSbP even though other, more credible, interpretations were available. Indeed, the paediatrician had to go to some effort to preserve the pattern by arguing that abnormal results were normal in paediatrics, thus ruling out test results that could be seen as confirming genuine illness, and that the pattern did not depend on any individual incident, so even if the mother could undermine such incidents, the pattern remained. In any event, the second premise in the argument is at least debatable.

The best that we can grant the two premises is, therefore, an uncertain status – and with the premises being uncertain, the conclusion cannot be certain. The question thus becomes, why was the narrative of guilt and dangerousness found persuasive when the syllogistic reasoning behind the narrative was so essentially uncertain? My view on this is that aspects of the narrative served rhetorical functions that helped mask or divert attention away from the underlying problems with the implicit syllogistic logic. It is my contention that what the argument lacked in substance was more than compensated for by what is termed 'narrative rhetoric'. This refers to those aspects or features of narrative that work together to construct a stable, persuasive story, whether or not the story is true or at least unstable. Indeed, some writers on literature argue for a rhetoric of fiction, that is, ways of persuading the reader that this is a good story (see, for example, Booth, 1961, and Chatman, 1978). I am not suggesting that any of the parties involved in constructing the story of guilt and dangerousness in P, C & S were acting in any way malevolently or duplicitously, or that there was any conspiracy to present a misleading, incomplete narrative – merely that the resultant text can be analysed rhetorically and found to manifest rhetorical techniques that served to bolster an argument that rested on shaky empirical ground and uncertain logical foundations.

Four features of narrative are particularly relevant here: clarity of the central action, level of detail, structure and cohesiveness and consistency.

Clarity of the central action

Bennett and Feldman (1981, p 41) state that stories organise information in ways that help the listener do three things: locate the central action, construct inferences about how surrounding story elements relate to the central action and be able to decide whether the inferences are compatible with each other and are sufficiently specific to lead to an unequivocal interpretation. Fundamental to this process, it seems to me, is the clarity of the central action, for if one is uncertain about the location and meaning of the central action, then inferences made on the basis of uncertainty and ambiguity may lead one to make inferences that do not point to the preferred interpretation. In simple situations it may be relatively easy to identify the central action; in complex situations it may be more difficult. There are two problems associated with clarifying the central action of complex situations: first, the complexity of the situation might make locating the central action difficult as there might be multiple locations from which to choose; second, the central action might itself be multiple in nature.

It is evident in literature across disciplines that multiple causation is recognised when dealing with complex situations. In political economy, for example, unemployment may be explained by a number of factors; in ecology, coral reef diversity is explained through multiple causes of regional history, frequency of disturbance and differential predation (see Schneider, 2009); in the field of human behaviour, multiple causation seems to be well established (see, for example, Cantor and Baume, 1999, on multiple causation in suicide); and in the social sciences, it is likely that multiple causation is the norm and models that allow for this are to be preferred (Robson, 2002). Multiple causes may also interact with one another, thus confounding easy clarification, making it more difficult to tell a cohesive and consistent, and thus persuasive, story.

One way of avoiding the narrative difficulties posed by multiple causation is to simplify the story by focusing on a single cause – in this case MSbP. MSbP as the central action allows for cohesiveness across connections – for example, the gastroenterological problems of the child in the US can be attributed to the MSbP behaviour of the mother rather than, say, a mixture of genuine illness, stress-induced illness as a result of being caught in the middle of very acrimonious disputes between the parents, poor reporting by the mother and, perhaps, even some elements of fabrication or exaggeration of symptoms (all of which can find some basis in the medical records and testimony of experts in the US proceedings).

Of course, this clarification of the central action runs into the danger of the fallacy of reduction – that is, crucial premises or qualifications are omitted from the argument (see de Witt Spurgin, 1993) – and as such, it is a technique that itself needs to be protected. I have indicated earlier how the trajectory of the plot was kept on track; here I explore how other narrative features contributed to protecting the central action, and we find this in the second rhetorical feature of narrative, the level of detail.

Level of detail

All stories are incomplete and all stories could be constructed differently. Take, for example, the rise in fan fiction in which individuals write supplementary episodes to existing stories or recent 'mashups' such as *Pride, prejudice and zombies* or *Sense, sensibility and sea serpents* in which new authors add to or rewrite existing works. The incompleteness or indeterminacy of any narrative rests, in part, in the level of detail provided by the author. A narrative is thus made more or less persuasive (or believable) according to not only what is included but also according to what is excluded from the final narrative – that is, the level of detail that is provided (see Bartlett and Wilson, 1982). If we have access to at least some of the material that could have been included but was not, then we might be able to determine how authorial choices might influence the persuasiveness of the text.

In P, C & S there is a mass of documentary material that did not find its way into the expert reports or the final social work recommendations to adopt the child outwith the birth family. If we take but a few examples we are able to see how the exclusion of such material might make the final text appear more persuasive than it would have been had the material been included.

Example one: MSbP as a diagnostic category. Fundamental to the case was the acceptance of MSbP as a valid and reliable diagnostic category. While this might, at first glance, seem self-evident, it is clear in the literature available at the time that there was no consensus about this (see, for example, Fisher and Mitchell, 1995; Morley, 1995; Baldwin, 1996; Bergeron, 1996; Blakemore-Brown, 1997, 1998; Ryan, 1997; Allison and Roberts, 1998). Indeed, at the time, and at the time of writing, this is still the case; MSbP did not appear in either the International Classification of Disease-10 of the World Health Organization or the *Diagnostic and statistical manual-IV-TR* of the American Psychiatric Association. Further, a number of court decisions in the US had dismissed MSbP as failing to meet the criteria for evidential reliability (for a discussion of this, see Baldwin, 2004). However, neither the contentiousness nor the conceptual and operational problems of MSbP were ever indicated by the local authority, the guardian ad litem or the various UK experts. Instead, MSbP was presented, misleadingly, as an uncontested, reliable and generally accepted diagnostic category. Similarly, the local authority, guardian ad litem and the courts glossed over the fact that three different (and not entirely reconcilable) versions of MSbP were deployed in P, C & S – those of the US prosecution psychiatrist (a psychiatric definition), the UK paediatrician (a non-standard paediatric version developed in his MD thesis) and the UK psychiatrist instructed by the local authority (a second psychiatric version) – each being different from the original formulation of MSbP by Meadow (1977). The rhetoric of MSbP as a valid diagnostic category was thus preserved (see Baldwin, 2005) and the problems of the first premise in the syllogism glossed over.

Example two: the selective presentation to the courts by social services and guardian ad litem of evidence concerning the parents. One example, among several, will suffice: even though social services had indicated in their notes regarding the contact sessions between the parents and the index child that the contact was 'exemplary' and the best that they had ever seen, such acclamation was not included in local authority reports to the court, and there is no indication that this had been taken into account when drawing up the plan for adoption. The inclusion of such positive parental behaviour and relationships would, I suggest, have acted to undermine the argument that the child might be at risk if left with them. The omission of detail contrary to the preferred characterisation avoided disrupting the alleged pattern of behaviour and family dynamics on which the case of MSbP, and the resulting plan for adoption, was based. In other words, such omission helped to maintain the second premise as valid by allowing for a more consistent pattern of behaviour to be presented.

Structure

If we examine the structure of the expert paediatric report we see the following: after the introductory remarks there are four sections dealing with the medical records. The first addresses the medical history of the mother's first child (approximately one page), the second section presents the medical history of the second child (approximately 13 pages), the third the medical history of the mother (approximately eight pages) and the maternity records regarding the mother and the unborn, index-child-to-be (approximately two pages). There follows a section titled 'Analysis' and then a conclusion in which the paediatrician makes his recommendations.

Such a structure is quite normal and, one might say, logical. It is, however, also rhetorical in that it presents material in a way that mirrors the argument that the mother had a pattern of behaviour: structure and content come together. Further, the structure lends the argument momentum: child one, child two, the mother, child three, analysis to conclusion and recommendations. The conclusion and recommendations appear almost inevitable outcomes and thus support the second premise and the conclusion of the underlying syllogism.

Similarly, the structure of each section can be viewed as rhetorically structured in that incidents that the paediatrician claimed were medically unexplained (part of the basis for his argument that the incidents were a result of the mother's behaviour) are interspersed with other incidents that are not remarked on but gain their significance from their positioning within the lists of other (supposedly) unexplained symptoms. Thus the reader is invited to interpret the latter, un-remarked on, incidents as potentially suspect (for this inferential approach to establishing connections between incidents, see Bennett and Feldman, 1981, pp 125ff). No evidence whatsoever is presented in the report that these incidents were in fact fabricated, and no claim was made that they were – the result being that the inference made by the positioning of these incidents is that there is a stronger pattern than if we removed these incidents, an inference that aligns with the second premise of the syllogism.

Cohesiveness and consistency

It has been demonstrated by Bennett and Feldman (1981, p 85) that as 'structural ambiguities in stories increase, credibility decreases, and vice versa.' Structural ambiguities, in Bennett and Feldman's work, refer to the clarity (or lack of) in the central action which gains its meaning from its setting and its resolution, the understandability of the connections made within the story and the consistency of these connections with the central action and one another. The consistency of these connections provides interpretative clues that support one interpretation and exclude all others (Bennett and Feldman, 1981, p 81). Thus, in Bennett and Feldman's research, it was found that a cohesive and consistent narrative was generally thought by participants to be true when it was not, and a fragmented, inconsistent or ambiguous narrative was thought false when, in fact, it was true. For Bennett and Feldman the structural aspects of the story become 'crucial to judgment in cases in which a collection of facts or evidence is subject to competing interpretations' (p 85). There are, of course, limitations to this, in that a story must bear enough relationship to the evidence to be considered structurally adequate, but even so, there is always freedom within those limits for competing stories to be considered so.

In the case of P, C & S in this light we have seen how the central action of the case, MSbP behaviour on the part of the mother, was clarified by omitting any discussion as to the validity or reliability of MSbP as a diagnostic category, the reduction of multiple causation to mono-causality, the omission of conflicting evidence and narrative smoothing. Further, attempts on the part of the mother to disturb the cohesiveness of the story (see earlier regarding the counter-arguments presented by the mother being interpreted in the light of MSbP rather than legal due process) were themselves recuperated into the story, thus moving the reader to the ineluctable conclusion that this was indeed a case of MSbP. The argument presented was, indeed, structurally adequate in that it was cohesive and consistent within its own parameters. If one steps outside those parameters, however – for example, by analysing the text rhetorically – one sees a different text, a text in which consistency and cohesiveness have been achieved at the cost of detail, negative character work, the protection of preferred narrators and, ultimately, logical form.

Earlier in this chapter I noted that all stories are incomplete and may be told differently. In the case of P, C & S in the domestic courts there were two primary narratives competing for acceptance: a narrative of guilt and/or dangerousness promulgated by the local authority and a narrative of innocence presented by the mother. In the European Court the competing narratives centred around human rights, with the mother arguing that the domestic proceedings had violated the provisions of the Human Rights Act 1998 and the UK government defending the actions of the local authority and the domestic courts as being legal and proportionate. The final outcome, the ruling that social services and the domestic courts had violated the human rights of both parents and child, is now the official and enduring narrative, authorised by the ECHR. Of course, the UK government could have appealed the decision in an attempt to establish an alternative authorised version, but they did not. Having been authorised and remaining effectively unchallenged, the official narrative of P, C & S is now one of state-perpetrated injustice. Had the mother not challenged the domestic courts, had she not found legal representation, had the ECHR found differently or had the UK government successfully appealed the decision, the 'truth' of the matter would have been very different.

Further reflections

At the beginning of this chapter I suggested that the lessons drawn from the analysis of this single case are transferable to other forms of alleged child abuse and other areas of social work. In closing this chapter I provide some examples of this. Such examples will, of necessity, be brief but are hopefully adequate enough to consolidate my suggestion.

Over the years there have been a number of cases in which narrative seems, initially, to have taken over as the basis of making judgments regarding alleged child abuse. In the late 1980s there were a number of alleged cases of abuse in which social services framed the narrative around the notion of Satanism. These resulted in the removal of children from their homes. In a number of these cases, just as with MSbP, we find significant ambiguity in definition; behaviour interpreted within the framework of the theory when it could, just as credibly, be interpreted in other, less suspicious ways; selectivity in the level of detail presented; and deference to and preference for certain narrators over others and many of the same evidential problems as with MSbP (see La Fontaine, 1998).

In cases where sudden infant death is framed as possible child murder we find elements of plot, trajectory, characterisation and rhetoric. In 1999, Sally Clark was found guilty of murdering her two young children. The narrative of guilt was constructed around the theory of the expert witness, Roy Meadow (he who also coined the term 'Munchausen syndrome by proxy', that 'one cot death is a tragedy, two is suspicious and three is murder'). This was the central action of the narrative and was then inferentially connected to events and behaviours:

> They [Steve and Sally Clark] agreed that Sally took time to settle up North until she made friends; that ideally they would have waited for a family until her legal career was established, but her biological clock was ticking and they decided on a family; that, yes, Sally did like to look smart and wondered whether she would get into her dresses again. All this trotted out by the Prosecution as a depressed mother, a career girl with a comfortable life style who did not want a family! Or, maybe the jury was swayed by inferences that Sally was rather too upset at the hospital; or after waiting four weeks she was rather too anxious for the autopsy report; or that she demonstrated Harry's collapse wrongly; or the exploitation of minor discrepancies on the sequence of events on the night. Inferences in the Prosecutor's speech but never supported by evidence. (Lockyer, nd)

Similarly we find configurations and reconfigurations of supporting characters in the form of paediatricians and pathologists, ambiguous findings in the medical records and questionable interpretations of those findings.

Sally Clark was not the only mother to be emplotted within a narrative of sudden infant death interpreted as child murder. Both Trupti Patel and Angela Cannings were initially found guilty of murder but later cleared of such following appeal court rulings that the expert evidence, again provided by Roy Meadow, was substantially flawed. In the case of Angela Cannings, the issues of narrative trajectory and the importance of narrative context are clearly indicated by Justice Judge, in his ruling in the Appeal Court, as having been a factor in the original conviction:

> It would probably be helpful at the outset to encapsulate different possible approaches to cases where three infant deaths have occurred in the same family, each apparently unexplained, and for each of which there is no evidence extraneous to the expert evidence that harm was or must have been inflicted (for example, indications or admissions of violence, or a pattern of ill-treatment). Nowadays such events in the same family are rare, very rare. One approach is to examine each death to see whether it is possible to identify one or other of the known natural causes of infant death. If this cannot be done, the rarity of such incidents in the same family is thought to raise a very powerful inference that the deaths must have resulted from deliberate

harm. The alternative approach is to start with the same fact, that three unexplained deaths in the same family are indeed rare, but thereafter to proceed on the basis that if there is nothing to explain them, in our current state of knowledge at any rate, they remain unexplained, and still, despite the known fact that some parents do smother their infant children, possible natural deaths.

It will immediately be apparent that much depends on the starting point which is adopted. The first approach is, putting it colloquially, that lightning does not strike three times in the same place. If so, the route to a finding of guilt is wide open. Almost any other piece of evidence can reasonably be interpreted to fit this conclusion. For example, if a mother who has lost three babies behaved or responded oddly, or strangely, or not in accordance with some theoretically "normal" way of behaving when faced with such a disaster, her behaviour might be thought to confirm the conclusion that lightning could not indeed have struck three times. If however the deaths were natural, virtually anything done by the mother on discovering such shattering and repeated disasters would be readily understandable as personal manifestations of profound natural shock and grief. *The importance of establishing the correct starting point is sufficiently demonstrated by this example.* (emphasis added) (Cannings, R v [2004] EWCA Crim 1 [19 January 2004])

In other areas of social work narrative can also play an important role. In the area of mental health narratives of risk, recovery, compliance, dangerousness and so on abound. Mental health assessments can thus be seen as exercises in characterisation. The narrative stance that is taken with regard to these is important – for example, are symptoms framed within a narrative of pathology or a narrative of 'a healthy self to find words and meanings that adequately express an individual's struggle with altered experiences' (Roberts, 2000, p 436)? Similarly, understanding how other disciplines might narratively frame mental distress may help social workers to critically evaluate such narratives and strengthen their abilities to construct counter-narratives (see Chapter 7 on narrative and mental health). Indeed, the General Social Care Council (2010) requirements for approved mental health practitioners that necessitates understanding and application of the social perspective on mental health emphasises the need for a counterstory to a dominant medical discourse.

In working with people living with dementia, again there are a number of possible narrative frames that can structure social work practice. The dominant meta–narrative about dementia is one of progressive decline often accompanied with a sense of therapeutic nihilism (see Jarvik and Winograd, 1988; Clark, 1995; Camp, 2006), but this is slowly being countered by different characterisations of people living with dementia individually through our understandings of non-linear, fragmented narratives and the meanings and structures therein (see Mills, 1998; Ryan et al, 2009) and politically with the move toward a citizenship model of dementia (see Bartlett and O'Connor, 2007; Baldwin, 2008b).

If, as I have argued, narrative features play an important role in the construction of persuasive narratives, it follows that an understanding of such features will open the door to evaluating those narratives in a more critical light. Understanding the importance and impact of plot, characterisation, trajectory and rhetoric allows us, then, to make decisions as to whether we think these are valid, legitimate and persuasive, or whether they mask fundamental problems within the narrative.

7

The narrative Self in
mental health discourse

by Brandi Estey-Burtt

It is usually taken as a matter of fact that biomedical knowledge is the dominant model that informs much of the discourse circulating about mental health in medicine, psychiatry and society at large. This model incorporates ideas of overarching medical beneficence and the primacy of scientific knowledge as it seeks to intervene in perceived medical problems manifesting in individual lives. Accordingly, this model displays certain assumptions about mental health, the relation of the Self to distress and appropriate methods of treatment. Several contemporary approaches to the Self have been discussed in Chapter 3 and I now turn to explore the Self in mental health discourse and its correlations with a theory of narrative, as well as its implications for social work practice in the field of mental health.

Meta-narrative of the Self

The *Diagnostic and statistical manual of mental disorders*, now in its fourth edition, with a fifth expected in 2013, concretises the dominant medical way of thinking about medical distress, categorising, classifying and indexing just about everything that can be perceived as 'abnormal' mental activity. The idea of crossing the line of normality underlies much of mental health discourse, including initial diagnosis and treatment. After it has been determined that normality has been breached, treatment consists of attempting to retrieve the normal Self that existed before the distress. This retrieval of the normal Self is an institutional form of the lay belief in restorable health: 'Yesterday I was healthy, today I am ill, but tomorrow I will be healthy again', a particular type of story that Frank (1995) calls the restitution narrative. In dementia, it is sometimes feared that 'once there is no narrative structure to the thoughts expressed by a body then there is no longer a self' (Thornton, 2003, p 362), and much of what passes for 'person–centred care' is exactly this attempt at retrieval, through reminiscence, life history, values histories and the like (see Baldwin and Estey-Burtt, 2013, forthcoming). This pursuit of restitution is embedded within an essentialist view of the Self wherein the Self is understood to be a coherent entity that exists independently of all that happens to it (see Chapter 3). Hence we get the 'essentialist idea that human beings are born with some intact personality, a psychic structure which renders some people prone to mental illness and others not' (Bainbridge, 1999, p 183). Sometimes the person him/herself does not realise what has happened, necessitating coercive, involuntary treatment designed to restore a state of mental normality. In such cases the lack of a coherent self-narrative is seen as part and parcel of acute psychosis (Holma and Aaltonen, 1995), and narrative discontinuity is, supposedly, 'markedly and overtly present' in cases of bipolar disorder, incipient schizophrenia and dissociative disorders (Wells, 2003, p 297). The restoration of narrative, and thus of the Self, then becomes the object of intervention: 'Narrative psychiatry, like narrative psychotherapy integration, recognises that the shaping of identity through narrative is a major tool for recovery' (Lewis, 2011, p 67).

In narrative terms, this assumption of the need for retrieval, restoration or restitution and the subsequent interventions become a story that adheres to the ideas of coherency, consistency and linear chronology, a unified narrative being equivalent to a unified Self. The mental distress a person experiences is seen as an unwelcome disruption of a person's long-term narrative as well as a fragmentation of the Self in the shorter term. Thus, stories deviating from this template represent not only inadequate narratives, but also a threat to a certain pragmatic model of narrativity. The imperative to reclaim the person who existed prior to the distress becomes a meta-narrative of medicine; in other words, it is taken up as the dominant model of narrative against which all others are measured. It thereby serves to frame individual stories within this meta-narrative of the medical model, with two key effects: (1) narrative dispossession, and/or (2) narrative foreclosure, which I discuss in detail below.

However, these narrative dictates have certainly not been without opposition. In his novel *If on a winter's night a traveler*, Italo Calvino (1981) challenges pre-conditioned notions of what a meaningful narrative should look like, how it should be structured and the themes it should examine. He explodes the concept of the coherent story as he describes the situation of a reader who is constantly prevented from finishing the succession of 10 novels he starts. Calvino thus builds fragmentation into the very structure of the novel to remind the reader that texts are always more than they appear, using this fragmentation as an invitation to explore what it means to read, understand and construct a story. Indeed, narrative coherency is being challenged increasingly in terms of theory, methodology and ethics (see Baldwin, 2006b; Hyvärinen et al, 2010), and Hyden (2010, p 36) states that 'broken' narratives, that is, narratives that do not adhere to conventional norms and expectations, are 'rather the rule than the exception in connection with illness narratives.'

If on a winter's night a traveler thus offers a useful framework to understand the inclusion of narrative approaches in mental health discourse within social work practice. The novel encourages alternative ways to tell stories and demonstrates the idea that fragmentation can open up new opportunities for understanding the Self rather than damaging it. *If on a winter's night a traveler's* endless circulations, flights of possibility, of which only some are developed, and inability to be fixed in a particular narrative style make this text seem oddly like a Self that has a multitude of opportunities but pursues only some of them, and then only some of these in any sort of complete fashion. No options are cut off, but, in Deleuzo-Guattarian terms, personal becoming is only limited by the imagination. This narrative approach resists colonisation by master or meta-narratives and therefore offers the potential to confront dominant models. Defying meta-narratives in this way enables the possibility of what Nelson (2001) calls counterstories, a means of recovering narrative and moral agency and asserting the power to tell one's story however one likes, and also a means of subverting meta-narratives (see Delgado, 1989; Ewick, 1995). I return to this below. These ideas therefore hold great significance for the practice of social work in the arena of mental health as critical social work seeks to uphold the individual self-expression of persons against prescriptive storylines imparted by biomedical attitudes to mental health.

Bearing this in mind, I turn now to the implications of narrative dispossession (see Chapter 2) and narrative foreclosure (Bohlmeijer et al, 2011; Freeman, 2011) prompted by the medical narrative of normality and a coherent Self mentioned earlier. I then argue that narrative, particularly in the form of counterstories, offers a compelling way to repossess and recover one's story.

Narrative and the Self

Narrative dispossession

Storytelling may be a ubiquitous practice, but it is not necessarily a simple one. The material construction of the story involving emplotment, character development, scene placement and such features that are recognisable to most people reveals only part of a complex process. These material aspects are always shaped by external considerations such as culture, class, gender, ethnicity, and so on, indicating that all stories, as Plummer (1994) rightly notices, are implicated in questions of power one way or another (see also Ewick and Silbey, 2003). Power influences what and how stories are told, as well as who listens to them. This also means that while some stories are celebrated and welcomed, others are deliberately discouraged from being told, with negative consequences for those whose stories are shut down. On a pragmatic level the effects of this could range from larger narratives that disenfranchise considerable groups of people to smaller, individual stories that cast a person as possessing moral or personal defects.

The two overlapping spheres that stories simultaneously enmesh tie into Nelson's (2001) analysis of the ways in which societal narratives socially and individually locate people and how such 'master' or meta-narratives may be resisted. For Nelson as well as Plummer, narratives permeate and are permeated by power. Power allows certain stories to be told while prohibiting others; moreover, it permits certain stories to be told in highly specific ways. For example, in research conducted by myself [CB], the narratives of mothers accused of MSbP abuse took very different forms depending on the forum in which they were being told and the power relations therein. Thus, the stories told in police interviews tended to be fragmented, partial and in line with the requirements of the interviewer while those told, for instance, in the research interview, tended to be stronger in terms of plot and more internally consistent. According to Nelson, power also influences perceptions of the moral agency of either groups or individuals, perceptions that we can see affect the types of stories that are told, such as those of the parents in Baruch's study (1981) who sought to establish moral adequacy in the face of threats to that adequacy by the perceptions of medical professionals. Nelson observes the triple consequences of this: (1) the limitation of social opportunity or resources for one group because of the actions and attitudes of a more powerful group; (2) the internalisation of negative opinions by a person in the invalidated group to the effect that they begin viewing themselves as morally incompetent, undeserving of self-respect or affirmation (Baruch, 1981, pp xii, 33), and (3) the recuperation of the alternative narrative into the language and understandings of the meta-narrative. In other words, those individuals whose stories do not align with meta-narratives may find themselves to be narratively dispossessed in a number of ways:

- they are either denied a narrative of their own (see, for example, McGranahan, 2010); or
- they may express themselves narratively only in terms determined by others, even to the extent of the language in which such narratives were to be told (see, for example, Poliandri, 2011, on the treatment of First Nations people in Canada); or
- they have their stories recuperated as further evidence of the correctness of the meta-narrative (see Baldwin, 2004, on the recuperation of narratives of innocence as indicative of guilt in cases of alleged MSbP abuse); or
- having expressed themselves in their own terms, they find their narratives interpreted within the language, style and understandings of the meta-narrative – witness, for example, Post (1983, p 212) on clinical interviews in psychiatry, 'The psychiatrist wishes to comprehend the patient and his disorder in terms of his own conceptual framework, whereas the patient and his friends have no theoretical interests in the matter' – in Good's words: 'One voice cannot exist alone because all voices possess form-shaping qualities upon the other' (Good, 2001, p x) – and when some voices become dominant others find themselves being shaped in hegemonic ways. Moral and narrative agency are here intertwined, imbricated in frameworks of power.

In terms of narrative, then, meta-narratives act in two ways: (1) they can narratively dispossess people, or (2) they can prompt narrative foreclosure. Narrative dispossession involves closing down opportunities for certain stories to be told, prohibiting narrative expression for persons or groups (Baldwin, 2006b). Narrative foreclosure marks the unwilling alignment of personal stories with social or institutional narratives, which has the effect of confining individual stories to ones already given in a certain setting (Freeman, 2000, 2010; Bohlmeijer et al, 2011).

Narrative dispossession in the area of mental health stems from the perpetuation of medicine's master narrative of scientific pre-eminence, professional benevolence and the maintenance of a certain notion of normality. Those viewed as mentally ill – people who break away from traditionally conceived normality either because of personal distress or individual desire – are often placed within the medical system and diagnosed with one of a myriad of disorders and pathologies (see, for example, Roberts, 2006). Narrative incoherence and fragmentation and erratic behaviour are interpreted symptomologically and prompt the conclusion that the person is incapable of a stable narrative identity (see Lysaker et al, 2003) and is, therefore, in need of 'fixing' (see also France and Uhlin, 2006). The medical diagnosis foregrounds an institutional narrative that precludes the individual's understanding and formation of their own story.

This scenario has frequently presented itself in psychiatric treatment, in which people can be put into a hospital or similar centre against their will and forcibly drugged or made to follow other treatment regimens. The disruption of narrative agency that follows the imposition of the medical narrative also manifests as a loss of agency in general, as the benevolence of medical professionals often completely curtails individual movement and choice once a person is in the system. David Oaks, Executive Director of MindFreedom International and a survivor of coercive psychiatry, describes his experiences in psychiatric institutions, including feelings of isolation, humiliation and distrust (2011). For Oaks, the tremendous power that medical professionals wield inhibits positive treatment outcomes by having such a damaging effect on the service user: 'When there is such a disparity in power, I have often found a silencing effect that can mute or distort the voice of the individual who finds him- or herself so shunned and discounted' (2011, p 192). This power disparity displaces or dispossesses personal narrative through the medical establishment's imposition of the biomedical narrative and unwillingness to provide a space for them to be told at all.

The service users Cohen (2008) interviewed offer an example of this. One service user, Yunas, had very harsh experiences of hospitalisation in which staff displayed excessive physical force, yet there was no one on the psychiatric team to whom he could tell this story. When the opportunity of home treatment presented itself, he encountered a different situation, where 'Home treatment service listen to what you've got to say. They work off what you've got to say' (quoted in Cohen, 2008, p 116). Although still feeling the after-effects of negative hospitalisation and coercive drug treatment, Yunas can now tell his story, although he admits that he is in the process of reforming himself after his experiences. Cohen remarks, with echoes of Stone (2008) and Barrett (1996), that 'Once in contact with the psychiatric system the [service user] narratives are muted in favour of the medical aetiology that talks of "illness", "diagnosis", "treatment", and "cure"' (Cohen, 2008, p 129). Perhaps the key word here is 'muted', as the user narratives are never given the chance to be both expressed and taken seriously, and are thus effectively dispossessed.

The other avenue that remains for people negatively affected by medical narratives of mental health resides in narrative foreclosure (Freeman, 2000). Although Freeman's concept of narrative foreclosure has been applied to people in later life, it can equally apply to mental health stories: 'with pre-scripted narratives of decline well in place, there appears little choice among the aged but to reconcile themselves to their narrative fate' (2000, p 81). In the medical narrative, a person's story becomes locked into the rhetoric of pathology and illness, and there seems to be no given alternative. Tekin (2011, p 365) describes this process well in writing that on the basis of a diagnosis of major depressive disorder, a person may:

> ... redefine her past experiences based on the descriptive framework established by the diagnostic schema, reassess the psychological and historical facts of her life in the light of the theory underlying her diagnosis, start to reevaluate certain events of her past as earlier symptoms of her mental disorder, and so on.... The alteration in the subject's autobiographical narrative may generate changes in her future plans, hopes, desires, anticipations, expectations, habits, as well as her relationships with others.

Furthermore, this storyline is reinforced by dominant cultural ideas about the nature of the pre-scripted narrative. The conviction that one's story is over or can only be lived according to certain terms 'may be a societal one as well, tied to prevailing images of development and decline or to the existence of cultural institutions that either fail to support the continued renewal of the life story or that actively promotes its premature ending' (Freeman, 2000, p 83).

For mental health service users, the diagnosis they are given by medical professionals becomes their narrative of decline that is then maintained by social and cultural images of that diagnosis. Barrett (1996) notes that once a diagnosis of schizophrenia is determined, the patient often learns how to tell their stories in light of this diagnosis. He describes one patient, Paul, who, through a series of interviews with medical professionals, 'thus learned to abbreviate his account, bring it to a focus on the clinically relevant features of schizophrenia, and omit what he knew the clinicians would find to be extraneous or ambiguous' (Barrett, 1996, p 135). Paul began to understand himself in terms of the label that had been placed on him. In this way, a person with schizophrenia is transformed into a schizophrenic and is judged according to current social and medical knowledge about schizophrenia (see Barrett, 1996) All too often this manifests as stigma directed towards a person perceived as having something wrong with them, consequences of the label given by the medical establishment as it ends up taking over the person as a whole, including their social life and identity.

Coppock and Hopton mention labelling theory in regards to hearing voices, noting that 'Labelling theory suggests that behaviour which is perceived as "abnormal" provokes others to define the individual(s) exhibiting such behaviour as deviant. This reaction leads "deviant" individuals to develop other "deviant" behaviours in an effort to cope with this stigmatisation, so that the label of "deviant" effectively becomes a self-fulfilling prophecy' (2000, p 83). Once again, the measure is of normality, and deviation from it produces certain social and medical consequences, including being put into the social category of deviancy. This in turn means that the 'deviant' person is assigned the narrative of deviancy, foreclosing their own and limiting their agency. Of course, this does not conclusively determine the social perceptions of those with mental distress, nor does it completely decide how they will subsequently perceive themselves. However, it certainly factors into the situation.

Mental health discourse's master/meta-narrative of normality and deviance thus excludes numerous smaller, alternative narratives, particularly those of the service users themselves. As Stone (2008, p 74) notes, 'The medicalised language of illness is a discourse sanctioned by power and hard to resist when one is in the limit-state of radical vulnerability.' The vulnerability heightened by mental distress makes it difficult to resist the stories imposed by the medical profession. Not only is the service user narratively dispossessed and unable to tell their own story, they also potentially go through a process of narrative foreclosure in which no new stories beyond that levied on them seem possible.

There are many such instances of the silencing, exclusion and even outright rejection of mental health user narratives. The power of which stories may be told and paid attention to lies clearly within the hands of the medical establishment and is thus demonstrably one-sided. The examples of the service users mentioned earlier illustrate the narrative dispossession and foreclosure that happens when such a power imbalance occurs and the meta-narrative of the dominant group is perpetuated to the disadvantage of the service user group. This demonstrably impairs the narrative and personal agency of the individual, making it difficult to break free of these structures.

This is not to deny the usefulness of the biomedical narrative for some service users. Many service users find the biomedical narrative useful in that it provides an understanding of their experience in culturally available terms and opens the door to accessing a range of support services, access itself dependent on the appropriate narrative. The difference here is that the biomedical narrative does not overstep its legitimate authority by becoming a meta-narrative that displaces or imposes itself on the self-determined narrative of the service user. Rather, it becomes one of several (or many) narratives within the wider narrative frame of the service user (see Baldwin and Estey-Burtt, 2012, forthcoming).

Just as narrative can dispossess and foreclose possibilities, so, too, can it provide opportunities to recover unique formations of Self and offer a means of resistance against meta-narratives. It is this empowering aspect of narrative to which we now turn.

Narrative recovery

As noted earlier, narratives are always subject to change and movement, even though some people or groups may want to lock them in for the long term. Furthermore, stories such as meta-narratives may be contested, challenged and overturned as marginalised groups marshal and deploy their own narratives. The process of narrative recovery or narrative repossession enables individuals as well as groups both to employ certain narrative strategies such as the counterstory as well as to embrace the very openness of narrative itself. Narrative becomes a way to resist the imposition of meta-narratives and a means to continually discover and shape the Self. Narrative therefore wields great power to transform identity on many different levels.

A crucial aspect of narrative recovery lies in what Nelson (2001, p 6) identifies as the counterstory: 'a counterstory – a story that resists an oppressive identity and attempts to replace it with one that commands respect.' In this instance, the construction of the narrative actively seeks to repair identity by affirming the worth and moral agency of the individual and also to countermand the oppressive meta-narrative.

The development and deployment of counterstories has achieved much success in areas that, like mental health, previously advocated a certain notion of normality and consequently marginalised the narrative identities of large numbers of people. The queer community, having experienced the brunt of oppressive stories on a social level as well as the denigrating effects of this on personal narratives, has since mobilised against the meta-narrative of heteronormative sexual and gender identity. Crip theory, developing insights from queer theory, has done similarly in regards to entrenched notions of able-bodiedness versus disability (see McRuer, 2006). For each of these 'the self is only a threshold, a door, a becoming between two multiplicities' (Deleuze and Guattari, 1987, p 249), and can be seen as examples of the rhizomatic Self, discussed in Chapter 3, in their development of ever-flexible, identity-constructing pathways that challenge the arborescence of much thinking about identity within mental health discourse.

In regards to mental health, what has been broadly called the service user movement has emerged as an empowering alternative to medical discourse. It is exceedingly diverse in the groups it represents, from the Hearing Voices Network for those seeking non-medical approaches to understanding and dealing with hearing voices, to the psychiatric survivors' movement that specifically protests against the use of coercive psychiatric treatment for mental distress. In the case of Mad Pride, large numbers of people have actively cooperated to reclaim the term 'madness' from the negative and stigmatised associations that have amassed throughout society, just as the queer community has fought to reclaim the word 'queer'. Also like the queer movement's work in sexuality and gender, Mad Pride has challenged entrenched societal notions of mental normalcy and rationality. Bainbridge (1999, p 181) reiterates this idea when he asks, 'Is there a universal entity called sanity in opposition to another universally recognisable entity called madness?' He, like Mad Pride, calls attention to the social construction of such concepts, particularly their placement in a binary opposition and their perpetuation through dominant forms of power.

As Coppock and Hopton (2000, p 50) note, 'It [the mental health users' movement] is informed by the principle that everyone has the right to be taken seriously and have their experiences recognised as meaningful. Crucially this includes the right to own and define one's own distress and to have a decisive influence in finding solutions to that distress.' The service user movement therefore represents the efforts of disenfranchised groups of people to deliberately resist the stories imposed on them while actively working to create empowering counterstories in which their experiences are recognised as valid, their equality in the service relationship acknowledged and their capacity for agency realised. The movement thus offers a way for service users to band together to effect systemic change.

But counterstories or recovery stories can also be mobilised on a more individual level, with productive change developing from careful attention to the very act of constructing a personal narrative. Such recovery narratives involve a work carried out on the Self. As Stone argues in relation to the writing activities of people diagnosed with psychosis, 'In writing, she recovers her speech, the closed-down self is reopened, and eventually she returns to the world' (2006, p 56). This act of construction alerts the individual to the processes of personal change and becoming. For example, O'Reilly (1997) examines the prominent role narrative plays in recovery for Alcoholics Anonymous (AA) participants. There is a simple structure that may be followed for those wanting to present their stories to the group, and it is this structure that aids the storyteller to perceive and enact positive personal change. It includes a brief introduction of the person and their troubles with alcohol before describing their desire to alter their patterns of behaviour. Recovery is in many cases tied to public storytelling, a visible space that supports the unique narrative potential of each person. Narrative is therefore viewed as an essential part of the ongoing process of recovery for AA members as well as many other addiction support groups.

As a counterstory to the medical meta-narrative of dependency, the AA narrative structure is useful for many people. This structure is, however, presented as an alternative template for the telling of a person's story rather than as creating an environment in which people can experience open-endedness, changeability and flexibility, what Gullette (2004, p 158) calls the 'thrill of narrative freedom'. Resisting the framing of the AA template – for example, denying the need for reliance on a higher power, the openness to the possibility of becoming a moderate drinker, or a refusal of a lifelong identity as an alcoholic – may be interpreted as not 'getting with the programme' and thus lacking commitment or being in denial.

Narrative development does not have to follow pre-scripted formulas, as in the case of AA. Indeed, narrative is ever changing and multiplicitous, and it is this fluid nature which allows it to work particularly well in aiding people with mental health troubles to repossess their own personal stories, countering the medical labels that all too often have subsumed their sense of Self. Such narrative dynamics works equally for groups as it does for individuals, promoting the right of everyone to tell their own stories and, moreover, to tell them in any form they wish. This also means that in counterstories as well as personal recovery narratives, recovery draws on sociality in order to be truly effective: narrative is a two-way endeavour which involves accountability to others and oneself as stories constantly intersect with one another. This aspect involves recognition that personal stories are always embroiled in other levels of storytelling such as the social and vice versa. The diversity of service users, the unique characteristics of each individual person and the relationships involved in shaping user stories may therefore be taken into account in a narrative approach. As Good (2001), cited earlier, points out, all voices have some shaping force on others, and so it is incumbent on us to take account of what impact our voice might be having, how it might be shaping others – the ethical interweaving of the Saying and the Said (how we tell things as well as what we tell of) discussed in Chapter 4.

The recognition of the importance and value of a person's story also aids in levelling the power relationship inherent in the professional/user encounter. The traditional model of paternalistic benevolence that has been the hallmark of clinical meetings can be reformulated into a more egalitarian understanding which supports the service user's developing understandings of her/his own mental distress through listening to the user's story, deconstructing the meta-narratives framing current understandings and becoming a co-author of the user's story through communication and support (see White and Epston, 1990). Any treatment course can therefore be decided on by both service user and professional as due consideration of the user's circumstances and desires informs treatment action. Therapeutic communities provide one attempt to re-work such relationships, grasping the idea that the professional is a dynamic part of the service user's story, and that 'understanding is owned by all and not seen solely to reside in professionals' (Campling, 2001, pp 365-66). Alternative therapies and coping strategies such as those outlined in Cohen (2008, pp 156-8) – including home treatment, engaging in artistic endeavours, sleep, religious activities, exercise, and so on – offer another way of respecting the user's preferences in regards to treatment.

There are thus a myriad of ways narrative can be used to challenge the meta-narrative of normality. It offers an unendingly creative means to understand and assemble the Self without necessitating recourse to stock narrative types or structures. It can therefore work on two levels: what Lewis (2011) identifies as a meta-approach, and a specific method. In other words, it can be employed both as a strategy and as a tactic: a strategy insofar as it offers a theoretical approach with which to guide diagnosis, professional/service user interaction and decision-making, and a tactic in the way it can be used as a specific type of therapy. Such a narrative approach to mental health does not portray psychiatry or other medical mental health services as a resolute evil, but rather admits the validity and usefulness of its methods and approaches for some service users. As Cohen admits, 'Of course we know psychiatry has had a chequered history and that some problems remain, but one cannot deny that people want and need psychiatric help from time to time' (2008, p 179). This may involve psychopharmacological drugs for one person or more holistic therapies offered outside of psychiatric institutions for another. Any approach is valid so long as it promotes the well-being and equality of the service user.

Narrative is not curative, however. It can prompt a fascinating process of self-discovery, but it does not promise miracles. In Ross David Burke's haunting description of his experiences of schizophrenia, *When the music's over* (1995, p 220), Burke recognises both aspects of narrative as he realises that even as he has learned about himself, he must go forward, although forward does not necessarily mean progress: 'My mind is full to the brim of the colorful words I uncovered in my idiotic nonsense, which amuses me and makes me glad I discovered myself by reading [his book] and seeing my thoughts.... I ride to heaven; or will I dwell on death?... I will walk away from the book into obscurity as a paranoid schizophrenic with a chemical imbalance in my brain.' After completing the writing of his story, Burke still suffered great mental distress and eventually committed suicide because of it.

The crucial thing about narrative that Burke understands is that, even though it may offer no cures, its importance lies in the fact that it is told. The power mechanisms at work behind narrative dispossession and foreclosure work to prevent the very telling of stories that do not match the official version. But, as the service user movement knows very well, the ability to tell stories restores a measure of power and agency to the one doing the telling. The story may not fix everything, but it emphasises the fact that people exist beyond the limiting terms of the medical label. It gives them a voice, an opportunity to verbalise their own existence (Stone, 2006). As Nelson (2001) argues, the voicing of such counterstories enables moral as well as narrative agency, or the capacity to articulate oneself as a moral being with attendant rights and capacity for action.

With these emancipatory aspects of narrative in mind, I now turn to social work's role in supporting the humanity, rights and individuality of the service user, and how the features of narrative mentioned earlier offer the possibility to strengthen these objectives.

Social work, narrative and mental health

It has already been established earlier in this book that narrative can have an immeasurable impact on social work practice by promoting a service user's basic rights to dignity, self-determination and overall well-being. In other words, narrative fundamentally supports social work values and principles (see, for example, BASW, 2002, and the discussion in Chapter 2). The substantial connections established between social work and narrative may now be concretely put into play by engaging the needs and stories of mental health service users. In this section, I outline conflicts social work has with the dominant medical model in understanding and dealing with mental health issues, social work's duty to mental health service users and the role of narrative in aiding social work's promotion of narrative agency and the narrative repossession of service users.

Social work frequently involves contact with medical professionals regarding the mental health issues of service users, with the biomedical model currently holding a monopoly on the discourse surrounding mental health. Consequently, there may be serious disjunctions between the viewpoints of both professions. Bainbridge (1999) comments on medicine's assessment of mental health, implicitly noting where social work stands: 'They really have no interest in looking at the relationships between health, mental health, social factors and the political economy, and at the extreme end see community mental health as a threat to professional identity and power. On the other hand, we have continuous models of sanity and madness which … try to break down the dominant-subordinate set of relations of the expert-consumer' (Bainbridge, 1999, p 191). These differences concurrently lead to issues of practice. As Bainbridge also observes, 'Vested interests of power underlying competing ontologies of sanity and madness inevitably lead to practice problems in relation to professional demarcation and territory' (1999, p 190). Morley and Macfarlane (2010, p 50) argue that in Australia, practice is not the only area of social work affected: the mental health curriculum for social workers also 'appears to have been co-opted into the medical colonisation of social work.' There are therefore serious reservations about the medical model's one-sided approach to mental health issues, as well as a desire to instead incorporate 'contextualised and holistic understandings of people's experiences' (2010, pp 46-7).

The idea of critical social work – social work that questions societal perpetuation of injustice and supports the humanity and dignity of the service user (see, for example, Parker et al, 1999; Morley and Macfarlane, 2010) – necessitates a certain positioning in regards to the mental health service user. Such a positioning includes basic assumptions about the role of the user in proceedings, the validity of their personal understandings of events and their expression of agency. Interactions should be informed by the goal of empowering the service user and respecting their individual situation. In this framework, social workers should not concern themselves with medical diagnoses as that would impose what Deleuze and Guattari identify as a line of articulation, or what I have earlier called narrative dispossession. It would work against social work's goal of upholding the uniqueness of the individual and their personal circumstances. Instead, social work must challenge the monolithic health system of psychiatry, seeking to support and enhance the empowerment of service users and their rights to self-determination. It should therefore be participatory in this regard, engaging with service users and not condescending to them from a position of power.

Accordingly, social work's emphasis on the social influences that shape an individual's life means developing approaches that can take account of such complexities. Narrative fits admirably here, although it requires a certain level of narrative literacy on the part of the social worker. It has the capacity to resist colonisation by the medical model, offering instead an unlimited potential for the support of the service user's health and well-being. Narrative is also remarkably flexible and adaptive and may therefore be appropriate for use with a diverse group of service users. It does not have to fit traditional examples of structure or plot, but is completely open to new modes of expression. To return to the analogy from Calvino's *If on a winter's night a traveler*, the story can morph into new and completely different stories at any moment, and fragmentation can be seen as an integral part of the narrative itself rather than as a sign of loss of capacity.

With a narrative approach, social workers can encourage the narrative repossession or recovery of service users as a specific goal of practice. As many service users display a need of reshaping their life stories into positive formations of Self, narrative aids in the recovering of agency as giving voice to one's story also means, once again in Stone's terms (2006), verbalising one's existence, or in McAdams' constructing a 'redemptive self' (McAdams, 2006). It constitutes something akin to what Stone also calls self-talk, 'by which the self, *in a willed and self-conscious movement* separates itself from the flux of existence and speaks to itself' (p 47; original emphasis). The story told may not necessarily produce any changes in outside power structures, although the counterstory can certainly achieve this, but it does help the teller iterate their sense(s) of Self and therefore discover a narrative agency or generativity in McAdams' terms, which may then extend to their everyday lives. Drawing from the example of the Gay Pride movement, individually asserting oneself as gay or lesbian may not overthrow societal negativity towards homosexuality; however, the action allows a gay or lesbian person to recognise their sexual orientation as a fundamental part of their narrative identity, which then affects how they perceive other stories constituting their day-to-day existence.

A measure of narrative literacy is needed by social workers to encourage this project of the Self. This means paying attention not only to the stories that are told by service users, but also how those stories are told. One should be familiar with traditional ideas of narrative such as plot, character, point of view and so on, which will emerge in many stories, but does not limit narrative expression solely to adherence to these conventions. Those experiencing severe mental distress may exhibit inconsistency, non-linearity and fragmentation as part of their narratives, but this does not lessen the meaning or legitimacy of their stories. One should also distinguish the external forces of power that shape the very telling of a narrative; the latter will be recognisable to social workers as the social influences on a person's situation. This means identifying the internalised frameworks of knowledge that everyone possesses and working to ensure that they do not impose on our understandings of each individual service user. For example, although the *Diagnostic and statistical manual* lays out expectations for certain diagnoses, the social worker should not let this medical framework force itself on the story told by the service user.

Further reflections

In using narrative as a constructive approach to mental health, social workers can forge a practice that respects the rights of the service user, even if it means running against the dictates of biomedical understandings. This enables social workers as well as service users to oppose the deleterious effects of narrative dispossession and foreclosure prompted by the imposition of the medical meta-narrative. Narrative recovery takes time, however, and demands flexibility and openness, although it surely holds out great possibilities for agency and self-understanding. The development of counterstories, be it on a group or individual level or a continuum between the two, has already proved to be successful among the mental health service users' movement, motivating positive change in mental health discourse and practice.

Meta-narratives of disability[1]

Authored with Mary-Dan Johnston

In his book of the same title, Marshall Gregory discusses how we are *shaped by stories*. For Gregory, what is at stake in the stories that we hear is the way stories construct the world, the way stories invite responses and the way that stories exert shaping pressure, because 'both the "knowledge" offered by stories and our seldom denied responses constitute kinds of practice, modes of clarification and sets of habits for living that, once configured and repeatedly reinforced, accompany us into real-life situations day in and day out' (Gregory, 2009, p 1). Now, although Gregory is discussing literature, there is no reason why other stories, cultural myths, discoursal frames, and so on should be excluded from exerting the same sort of shaping pressures. These sorts of stories, that is, non-literary stories, are often termed what we have elsewhere identified as meta-narratives. In Chapter 1 we briefly suggested that, along with Nelson (2001), we can understand meta-narratives as summaries of socially shared understandings. In this chapter we explore a number of such meta-narratives as they pertain to disability, and how these narratives understand and frame disability, setting the boundaries for what can be told about disability and how it can be told. For example, in discussing the stem cell debate in Australia, Goggin and Newell (2004, p 51) argue that 'there is a consistent emplotment concerning the social tragedy of disability and delivery from the catastrophe for individuals', a view of disability that cannot understand such alternative narratives of disability bringing benefits and joy (see Power, 2009; and see later), or the desire to become 'disabled' through voluntary amputation of a healthy limb (see, for example, S.H., nd).

Understanding such meta-narratives of the body is important as, in social work practice, we encounter a diversity of bodies – black, brown, white, male, female, young and old – and bodies that resist such categorisation. We know from our own experiences that our bodies shape how it is that we are treated in the world – they help to make sense of our past and determine our possibilities for the future. However, this power is not inherent within bodies, but is rather the outcome of social processes that have coded certain types of bodies in specific ways. In this chapter, we are particularly interested in the development of the notion of so-called 'broken bodies' (Clapton and Fitzgerald, 2012, p 2), which leads us to explore the concept of disability.

Historically, bodily difference has been a major factor in the creation of social structures (Clapton and Fitzgerald, 2012). Through the definition of some types of bodies as 'normal', those bodies that fail to conform to the standard are defined as 'Other'. What counts as 'normal' continues to be defined by those in privileged positions without the consultation of those who have themselves lived the experience, and social policy, funding and legislation based on such definitions directly reflect vested interests (see Goggin and Newell, 2004). These are the meta-narratives that continue to shape our understandings of our bodies and the possibilities they afford us. Recently, however, many theorists have challenged the standard view, using their own experiences to reveal the incompleteness of other models of disability.

The meta-narratives constructing the cultural, social and political spaces within which disability can be understood have changed over time, shifting with historical developments and changes in the economic forces of society. For example, there has been a significant shift from early moralistic understandings that framed physical or mental impairment as either a curse from the gods or a blessing in disguise to more contemporary narratives that locate disability in the social environment or even as an untapped market for consumer goods (Haller, 1995).

In order to make sense of these changing understandings, we must first remember that the experience of disability is not the same as the experience of impairment. Generally speaking, impairment can be defined as 'an injury, illness, or congenital condition that causes or is likely to cause a loss or difference of physiological or psychological function', while disability can be defined as 'the loss or limitation of opportunities to take part in society on an equal level with others due to social and environmental barriers' (Northern Officer Group Report, 2002, p 1).

In this chapter we explore how the meta-narratives of disability developed, and how they function. We begin by providing an historical overview of the three main meta-narratives of disability, all of which take the location of disability as their central task. The religious and medical-genetic meta-narratives construct the individual as the locus of disability, while the social model understands disability as a condition located in the social environment. Following this, we explore counterstories, stories that seek to refuse, repudiate or replace these meta-narratives (see Nelson, 2001) with other identity-forming narratives based on inclusion. With each meta-narrative and counterstory, we describe the potential for the constraint and liberation of individuals. Finally, through our exploration, we assess the implications of each of these meta-narratives for social work practice in an attempt to arrive at an understanding of disability that is in line with the narrative element of social work values and a narrative view of the Self (see Chapters 2 and 3 respectively).

In order to understand how disability agendas and resulting political actions can work to the benefit of stakeholders in the disability community, we must take note of transforming narratives of disability.

To begin, it must be said that many scholars of note (Tremain, 2002; Metzler, 2006; Goodley, 2007b) draw attention to an important issue at the outset of their work on disability. They point explicitly to the fact that the term 'disability' is a frail concept – that is, it is problematic in what it suggests (Metzler, 2006). It provides those interested in the historical treatment of individuals with impairments as well as with the social reaction and explanation of those impairments little with which to work. The term disability is historically contingent, and we must be wary of imposing our contemporary meanings, definitions, connotations and understandings on the world that we hope to explore, taking care as we sift through the historical record for evidence of the attitudes and understandings of the past. Whether we want to discover how the religious, social or medical meta-narratives emerged, we must bear in mind that the concept of disability is one that we bring to the table, and may not be appropriate to describe the phenomena observed (Metzler, 2006).

Religious meta-narrative

There have always been different types of human bodies. Long before the discovery of the human genome or the development of the prosthetic limb, human difference was recognised and made sense of in a way that was relevant to the social, economic and political context of a particular time and place. In some contexts, certain types of human difference took on a particular meaning, where in others they may have escaped classification. For centuries before the Enlightenment, the moral authority of the Church was paramount throughout Europe, and it is thus unsurprising that the Church and its doctrines had a significant impact on how impairment and disability were then understood. In this section we focus on the religious model of disability dominant in much of the Western world through the late Middle Ages, addressing the consequences of this model for those living with impairments.

Metzler (2006) notes that in the Christian tradition, there are two distinct approaches to impairment. The first, characteristic of the Christian Old Testament, connects 'the character of a person, sin and physical imperfection, in that those who disobey the divine law are afflicted with various illnesses and impairments, such as blindness and leg ailments' (Metzler, 2006, p 39). The second approach comes when Jesus, whose ministry is defined by healing, emerges as the central figure. This approach is gentler, not eliminating the possibility of a relationship between impairment and sin, nor positing one absolutely. Both these approaches are located within the ongoing story of God's chosen people, their relationship with God and their ultimate salvation. Although such scholars as Wheatley (2010) and Covey (2005) have equated impairment with sin, Metzler challenges this view, noting that there are several instances of disability referenced in the Bible where no mention is made of sin:

> Many instances of the healing of impairment or illness occur in the New Testament where the status of a person as sinner or repentant is not mentioned at all – the question of sin in connection with the healing of an afflicted person is not always an issue. For example, Jesus heals possessed people, a deaf and a mute man, a blind man, and the

blind beggar Bartimaeus – none of whom are asked about their sins.
(Metzler, 2006, p 42)

Metzler asserts that the connection between impairment and sin was constantly being revised, and she argues that the relationship should not be conceived of as unchanging and static.

According to Wheatley (2002), the Church's initial interest in the impaired and the unwell grew out of Jesus's role as a healer and worker of miracles. In the Bible, one of Jesus's most notable encounters with an impaired person is described in John 9, when he meets a blind man on the road. When his disciples inquire as to who is to blame for the man's blindness, Jesus applies a clay of dust and spit to the blind man's eyes, telling his disciples, 'Neither hath this man sinned, nor his parents; but that the works of God should be made manifest in him' (John 9:3). This story betrays a New Testament Christian understanding of the physical blemish as the site for divine intervention, rather than as a mark of sin (Wheatley, 2002).

However, in spite of the encounter where Jesus dispels the assumptions of his disciples, the connection between sin and impairment is revisited later that chapter. Wheatley points to another passage in John where Jesus alludes to the possibility that something worse could happen to the (formerly) blind man. Jesus says, 'Go and sin no more, lest some worse thing happen to thee.' The Fourth Lateran Council of 1215 interpreted this passage as a warning against having a tarnished soul at death's door, again locating impairment in the religious narrative of salvation. The Council recommended that all doctors attending the ailing should first direct their patients to 'the physician of souls' in order to have their 'spiritual health restored to them … the application of bodily medicine may be of greater benefit, for the cause being removed, the effect will pass away' (Wheatley, 2002, p 195). For Wheatley, this interpretation of impairment is the basis for the religious narrative. When spiritual health becomes necessary for physical health, the Church has an enormous amount of power when it comes to defining health, illness and impairment, and the discursive authority of the Church strengthened the religious narrative as the way to understand disability in the early modern period and the Middle Ages.

People living with impairments who hoped for a cure and an easier life would therefore have little choice but to submit to the religious discipline of the Church. Economically, Wheatley (2010) suggests that this arrangement would have been lucrative, as the Church would benefit financially from having a number of followers essentially tethered to the institution who would submit willingly to the discipline it required and perform the work it demanded. In this way Wheatley problematises this meta-narrative as the discipline of the Church puts serious constraints on the human freedom of impaired people, preventing alternative narratives through the threat of eternal damnation. As such, this narrative discipline illustrates Plummer's (1994) view of stories in the wider world reflecting and constituting power relationships, and the ways in which spaces are opened up for some stories and closed down for others. It also suggests that there were cracks or niches within the religious narrative that would allow for counterstories to gain purchase. For Nelson (2001) counterstories can gain such a grip in the gaps between what is claimed by the meta-narrative and the lived experiences of individuals, perhaps in the discrepancy between righteous people being inflicted with some form of disability or obvious sinners living long and healthy lives. Further, with the development of medicine, disability need no longer be seen as the result of an individual's sin, and there are possibilities for cures other than through prayer, repentance and grace, thus opening a space for an alternative narrative to be developed and heard.

Metzler (2006) suggests that the religious discourse of disability shares many traits with the medical discourse of disability, perhaps because in those times, no great distinction existed – those who studied 'science' would also have been versed in theology and philosophy. Metzler suggests that imposing our modern distinction between the disciplines distracts us from the dynamic relationship between religion and science at the time. It makes sense, then, that Wheatley takes up Linton's definition of the medical model of disability, suggesting that the word 'medical' might simply be replaced with the word 'religious':

> Briefly, the medicalization of disability casts human variation as deviance from the norm, as pathological condition, as deficit, and, significantly, as an individual burden and personal tragedy. Society, in agreeing to assign medical meaning to disability, colludes to keep the issue within the purview of the medical establishment, to keep it a personal matter and "treat" the condition and the person with the condition rather than "treating" the social processes and policies that constrict disabled people's lives. (Linton, quoted in Wheatley, 2010, p 8)

It is the medical model of disability that we look at now, drawing out its effects in modern society and providing specific examples of its operative concept of disability.

Medical meta-narrative

The medical model of disability emerged as the influence of the Church waned in the period following the French Revolution, and it brought with it a number of important changes in productive and cultural spheres. Although the medical model shares many things with the religious model in terms of the effect it has on individual subjects, it also presents its own unique challenges, which we discuss below. The key features of the medical model are: (a) its focus on the individual body as the site of pathology, and (b) its determination to find a 'cure' that can be applied to that pathology. The employment within this model, as adapted from Goggin and Newell (2004, p 51), is sequenced thus:

1. The life of an individual or several devalued individuals is portrayed as a tragedy.
2. A technology is represented as delivering the individual(s) from disability.
3. Securing the technology means that the disability has been dealt with – the individuals no longer have to be 'disabled'.

In this section we examine the emergence of the medical meta-narrative, its implications for people living with physical and mental impairments and its relevance to disability today.

The medical meta-narrative supplanted the religious one at a particular historical moment. As wealth was transported from the colonies to the home countries, investment in large-scale production increased and peasants were forced off of the land and into the cities as a result of the Enclosure Movement (Redford, 1976). Previously, domestic work and economic production had both taken place primarily within the home, where people with different bodily abilities would have been largely cared for and accommodated by their families (Clapton and Fitzgerald, 2012). As wage labour became increasingly common, the meaning of physical and mental impairment began to change. In a world where work was being transferred from the home into the factory, a new kind of discipline was imposed on production: the clock (Braverman, 1974). Those who could not adjust their own work to the pace of factory production would suffer. In an economy where labour was abundant, who were not 'fit' for such work would therefore be cast aside in favour of a more capable or desperate individual (Clapton and Fitzgerald, 2012).

This environment – the discipline of the factory combined with an increasing focus on rational, scientific thought – was one in which a medical narrative of disability could find strong roots. Medicine as a discipline and practice had been developing and gaining trustworthiness, and as the Church lost credibility amidst secular ideas circulating in the late 18th century, it left a power vacuum into which the medical establishment could step. It is important to note that although the institutions occupying the position of power changed, it was little more than an administrative shift – the power structure remained fundamentally the same. While the bodies of people with impairments had been singled out by the Church and designated as sinful, those same bodies were singled out in much the same way by the medical establishment, who defined them as functionally rather than spiritually broken (Clapton and Fitzgerald, 2012).

The medical meta-narrative is still strong today, encapsulating as it does social and cultural fears and aspirations and the continuing belief in technology as a means to address health and social needs. Today, in this narrative, impairments are understood for the most part as technical problems with technical solutions; if they can be 'fixed' by medical science, they *should* be (Clapton and Fitzgerald, 2012). It is generally assumed that a deaf person will want hearing aids or that someone without one of their limbs will want a prosthetic replacement, even though this may not always be the case, and within the medical meta-narrative, the primary and preferred way to alleviate disability is to intervene on the individual's body and act on the impairment. From this perspective, the person with the impairment is *disabled* by his or her body – the problem is located on the level of the individual (Shakespeare and Watson, 2002). Accordingly, 'disability' is seen as a tragic or pitiable medical reality. If a treatment exists to make the bodies of those with impairments more 'normal', the impaired are expected to drop everything in order to be 'treated'. Despite attempts to frame medical intervention as inclusive and respectful of human difference, this expectation betrays the position of the 'disabled' as the Other (Clapton and Fitzgerald, 2012).

If those who are impaired fail to subject themselves to procedures that are often invasive, expensive and potentially dangerous, they are thought to be too proud for their own good, and often just plain stupid – after all, only someone who lacked common sense would wilfully stay in a 'broken' body. For Goffman (1963), this attitude is the result of the social *stigmatisation* of disabled individuals, who are seen as 'shamefully incomplete' if they remain 'uncured' (Wheatley, 2010). Disability advocates who argue against this view claim that they are tired of being regarded as deficient when simple changes could be made to make their lives simpler at no great expense.

The medical meta-narrative privileges a very narrow definition of human freedom over all other considerations, paramountcy being given to the freedom to work and be productive (within a society where those terms are quite limited in scope). Although some interventions on impaired bodies can make it easier to participate in the world in this way, which can alleviate the distress experienced by some disabled people, what this type of intervention really amounts to is shaping bodies to fit the machinery of the productive sphere (Foucault, 1977). While there are many who argue that medical interventions dramatically improve the quality of life of people with impairments, there are some cases where 'fixing' the impairment can fundamentally alter the life of the individual concerned. As Garland–Thomson eloquently summarises:

> The ideology of cure directed at disabled people focuses on changing bodies imagined as abnormal and dysfunctional rather than on exclusionary attitudinal, environmental and economic barriers. The emphasis on cure reduces the cultural tolerance for human variation and vulnerability by locating disability in bodies imagined as flawed rather than social systems in need of fixing. (2006, p 264)

We can see the power of the medical narrative at work in the following example, in which parents of twins with Down syndrome attempt to challenge the desirability of a cure for their children's condition.

In 2010, a parenting blog on the *New York Times* website published a story about a recent scientific development coming out of Stanford University. It seemed that researchers there had developed a 'cure' for Down syndrome. The 'cure' (norepinephrine injected into the brain) would, allegedly, improve the neural memory of children with Down syndrome, allowing them to learn and advance cognitively at a rate closer to their peers without the condition. The blog published a link to the Stanford research along with a blog post by Jenn Power, a mother of twin boys with Down syndrome, who expressed her discomfort with the notion that Down syndrome needed to be 'cured'.

The backlash Power received in the comments section of the blog was intense, with some readers questioning her aptitude as a parent and others accusing her of being cruel, inhumane and selfish. Some suggested that she was using the impairment of her children to feel better about herself, while others implied that Power's children were no more than 'therapy animals' (Belkin, 2010). In her original post, Power made it clear that she was not interested in altering the personalities of her children. She highlighted the benefits of living with Down syndrome and the joy that her children had brought into her own life, as well as the lives of others. Problematising the medical model, she wrote:

> In the debate surrounding disability – prenatal screening, euthanasia, etc – there is an assumption that we all agree on a definition of what is good, what is better, what is the ideal. Who decided that smarter is better? Who decided that independence takes precedence over community? Who decided that both the individual and the society are better off without Down Syndrome? I would assert that something important is lost as our genetic diversity diminishes. I would also assert that people with disabilities may not themselves choose to be "cured". Bioethicist and disability activist Gregor Wolbring, who happens to have no legs as a result of the effects of thalidomide, asserts that, if given the choice, he would want to remain "disabled". He feels it gives him an evolutionary advantage, even, as it allows him to weed out the "jerks" who treat him differently as a result of his disability. He poses the compelling question, "What exactly is the problem? Is the problem that I have no legs, or is the problem that I live in a leg-dominated society?" Similarly, what exactly is the problem with Down Syndrome? Is the problem that my boys have a low IQ, or that they live in an IQ dominated society? (Power, 2009)

Power's husband also weighed in on the issue, responding to the medicalisation of developmental impairments:

> One of the folk wisdom expressions I learned at [my father's] knee is this one: "If all you have is a hammer, everything looks like a nail." I would paraphrase it thusly: "If what you have is medical training, everything looks like a disease." This whole debate about a "cure" for Down Syndrome is analogous to the much more widespread question of pre-natal testing and abortion. In most developed nations, the abortion rate for fetuses with Down Syndrome is around 90%. Since people with congenital disabilities are not generally born to like parents

(in terms of marginalized groups and politics within the family, people with disabilities have a lot in common here with people who are homosexual), parents in this situation are extremely dependent on their doctor's advice. But there is nothing in the doctor's medical training that puts them in contact with a non-disease-oriented understanding of disability. This dramatic eugenic shift is taking place in our society right now, and neither people with Down Syndrome, nor the people close to them have any voice in it. (Donham, 2009)

Both Power and Donham responded to the medical model on behalf of their children and others in their lives to show how people with impairments are characterised through focusing exclusively on their disability without taking other aspects of their lives into consideration. The frames and schema of medicine, rooted in technology, science and an ablest economy, effectively marginalise and almost silence alternative narratives – and as such can be seen as narrative strategies, creating the space for the telling of a single narrative and closing down not only the space that other narratives might inhabit but also de-legitimising alternative narratives such as Power and Donham's.

While there have been some successes in creating more accessible geographical, cultural and social spaces for people with physical impairments, by and large, however, it is the medical meta-narrative that continues to be the dominant discourse in the debate on disability. Just as 'Othering' as the religious model, the medical meta-narrative does not give voice to people living with impairments but relegates them to the status of simple carriers of a disability, expecting that people with impairments will willingly re-arrange their lives in order to accommodate their impairment and gracefully accept the burden placed on them (Clapton and Fitzgerald, 2012). However, it is important to note that physical and mental 'normalcy' were constructed without the consent of those being plotted on the Bell Curve (the pre-determined distribution pattern of physical and mental characteristics that shapes what constitutes normality) (Davis, 2006, p 4), and thus the medical meta-narrative can be seen as a form of epistemic rigging (Nelson, 2001) that naturalises the disabled body and thus justifies the meta-narrative's worldview and the actions based on it. In this way it is clear that the medical meta-narrative and its various cultural incarnations is fundamentally anti-democratic; it must continue to be enforced through various forms of discipline (from the regulation of the Self to coercion by the courts) because it is not an authentic explanation – it does not arise from the lived experiences of impaired individuals. In a world where only 'docile bodies' are acceptable, cultural hegemony ensures that images of the 'norm' percolate continuously, rendering the reminder of one's supposed incompleteness inescapable (Garland-Thomson, 2002).

Alternative narratives about disability have arisen not only in individual cases of resistance to the medical meta-narrative but also as alternative meta-narratives. A good counterstory, according to Nelson (2001, p 183), is one that aims 'to free the entire group whose identity is damaged by an oppressive master narrative.'

Alternative narratives, such as the social meta-narrative, seek to challenge the 'deprivation of opportunity and infiltrated consciousness' embedded within the medical meta-narrative. In seeking to displace the medical meta-narrative, the social one challenges the stock plots and characterisations of disabled people as individually deficient and limited, arguing for their replacement by a narrative in which social, cultural and environmental factors act so as to disable some individuals and not others.

Social meta-narrative

From the overview of both the religious and medical models of disability, we can see that disabled people have faced oppressive conditions for hundreds of years. Although their material conditions have improved with the institution of social and financial benefits and the extension of publicly funded healthcare to disabled people in some countries, the stories told about disability have historically focused on the individuals affected, whether by explaining disability in terms of moral failing or biological deficit (Shakespeare, 2006a). However, in the last 30 years, movements initiated by disabled people around the world have challenged the medical meta-narrative in favour of a social one that problematises the social relations and structure that build an ableist world. Although there were and continue to be many different approaches to disability that take the social as their primary terrain, the 'social model of disability', coined by Oliver in 1983, has come to dominate the social discourse on disability (Shakespeare, 2006b).

The social meta-narrative emerged out of the work of a number of disabled persons' political groups, some with reformist aspirations while others were more radical in purpose. Shakespeare (2006a) argues that the Union of Physically Impaired Against Segregation (UPIAS) was particularly influential, their 1974 policy statement making them one of the first groups to identify disabled people as an oppressed group. In a 1975 discussion document on the 'Fundamental principles of disability', UPIAS claimed it was society that disabled people:

> Disability is something imposed on top of our impairments, by the way we are unnecessarily isolated and excluded from full participation in society. Disabled people are therefore an oppressed group in society ... [disability is] the disadvantage or restriction of activity caused by a contemporary social organisation which takes little or no account of people who have physical impairments and thus excludes them from participation in the mainstream of social activities. (UPIAS, 1975, quoted in Shakespeare, 2006a, p 198)

Shakespeare explains that this definition of disability is particular to the British social model. It rests on three important points:

- Impairment and disability are not the same thing. Impairment is the actual physical condition, which is, as Shakespeare says, 'individual and private', while disability is the social exclusion borne of social forces that are 'structural and public' (2006a, p 198).
- Disability is seen as constructed rather than as a matter of personal deficit. Accordingly, interventions on disability should be aimed at the public level, through legislative and regulatory actions.
- There is a dichotomy between disabled people and non-disabled people, who, either acting alone or through their organisations, often participate in the oppression of disabled people (Shakespeare, 2006a, p 199).

From an overview of these three principles, we can see how certain types of political actions would be encouraged, identifying structural factors as the cause of disability and arguing for the elimination of those structural barriers. In so doing, there has been a potential fault-line in the developing narrative as a counterstory to the medical meta-narrative. Nelson (2001, p 182) depicts this as the bathwater story, that is, in dislodging the opposing meta-narrative it also dislodges too many other understandings. In the extreme case, where the disabling trait is viewed as a neutral human variation, Nelson argues that there would be no reason for publicly funded healthcare to directly address the trait even if that trait were psychologically or physically distressing to the individual. Fortunately, the social meta-narrative has, so far and on the whole, steered clear of such an approach, and has focused on possible approaches involving services conceived of and run by disabled people for disabled people, legislation aimed at enshrining the rights of disabled people specifically and enforcement of new regulations and laws; in other words, a rights-based or citizenship approach to disability.

The central action within this social meta-narrative is intervention at the social level, and roles and characters are allocated in relation to that action – see Shakespeare's third point above. This central action often takes the form of political advocacy for protections to disabled people – the creation of a contract that guarantees appropriate compensation for the existing discrimination that they face (for example, preferential hiring, medical and social benefits, representation on public decision-making bodies, consultation on issues that will involve them, and so on) (Shakespeare and Watson, 2002).

Although this narrative has certainly helped create a space in which the voices of members of the disabled community can be heard, and has resulted in policy victories and more overall awareness on the issue of disability, critical disability theorists such as Smith and Sparkes (2008), Watson (2002) and Goodley (2010) suggest that the social meta-narrative is out-dated and even damaging to the cause of disabled people. Rather than eliminating the essential construction of the disabled as 'Other', the social meta-narrative is built on that Otherness. As Clapton and Fitzgerald note, 'rather than seeking to dismantle the entire concept of disability, [the social meta-narrative] actually relies upon such a construction to support its claims for rights and entitlements' (2012).

Rather than continuing to frame the conversation about disability in terms of what kinds of protections can be secured for 'the disabled', Shakespeare and others (Wyller, 1997; Smith and Sparkes, 2008) argue that the movement must step away from making a sharp distinction between disability and impairment and begin to understand those concepts on a spectrum. Shakespeare and Watson hope that the eventual outcome of this perspective will be the acceptance of 'the ubiquity of impairment' for all humans, breaking down the false dichotomy between the able-bodied and the disabled – the normal and the 'Other' (2002, p 26).

A rhizomatic approach to disability

Having provided an assessment of the relative strengths and limitations of what are currently thought to be the main models of disability, we now turn our focus to an alternative. What we have noticed in our review is that the religious, medical and social meta-narratives have been limiting in their scope. By confining the understanding of disability to the moral, medical and social realms, each fails to provide a framework for understanding the complexity of the lived experience of disability. While the religious and medical models located disability in the individual, the social model simply turns the table, locating disability in the social instead, and thus, in Deleuzo-Guattarian terms, substituting one arborescent form of thinking and identity construction with another (see Chapter 3 on the rhizomatic Self). Shakespeare and Watson (2002) note that each of the models favoured in the past helped move forward the discursive struggle to account for the experiences of disabled people, and they suggest that we have again come to such a time when the limitations of the dominant paradigm become clear.

While the medical and religious models fall squarely within the bounds of methodological individualism, the social model has been accused of what we will term 'methodological collectivism'. Although the two sets of approaches put a different focus at their respective centres, neither can account for the complexity of the lived experience of disabled people, which, as Wyller (1997) argues, must take into account both the bodily reality of the person in question and the material and social structures in which they are inevitably embedded. In framing the lives of disabled people in line with a pre-given framework of how disability is to be understood, each of these meta-narratives territorialise the lived experiences of disabled people through lines of articulation based in abstract frameworks of understanding. For example, from the perspective of the other three meta-narratives explored in this chapter, disability is often construed as a force that interrupts subjectivity or personhood. In the medical and religious narratives, the interruption is located at the level of the individual, while in the social narrative, the same interruption is located in the societal structures that disabled people live within. Although these meta-narratives claim to be fundamentally opposed to each other, their commonality is what makes them both inadequate for understanding the experiences of disabled people. While one isolates the individual, the other isolates the system within which they live, giving no space to the person that we are allegedly interested in to explain their own situation.

What we need, then, is a perspective on disability that looks not only at the disabled individual and the disabling environment but also at desire, possibility and resistance (see Goodley, 2007b). This is to be found, we believe, in the notion of rhizomatics – the ongoing work of becoming (Deleuze and Guattari, 1987) – and the philosophy of Emmanuel Levinas that helps to make clear how the imposition of the religious, medical and social models on disabled people can in fact constitute an act of violence (Robbins, 2000). Referring to the Self's confrontation with the Other, Levinas (1961) notes that when the two encounter each other, the Self can make one of two choices. One, the Self can 'attempt to impose itself onto the Other, by insisting on the correctness, applicability and acceptance of its worldview, interpretations, concepts, definitions, beliefs, attitudes, and behaviours' (Baldwin and Estey–Burtt, 2012, forthcoming). As McRuer (2006, p 9) puts it: 'A system of compulsory able-bodiedness repeatedly demands that people with disabilities embody for others an affirmative answer to the unspoken question, "Yes, but in the end, wouldn't you rather be more like me?"' Alternatively, the Self can respond 'with a sense of responsibility and obligation toward the other in all her/his otherness' (Baldwin and Estey–Burtt, 2013, forthcoming).

In entering deeply into the encounter with the Other, the Self may see that the Other represents nothing about the Self and at the same time everything. The complete vulnerability of the Other is ultimately recognised by the Self, who comes to understand the Other's vulnerable call as a plea, 'Do not kill me' (see Benso, 1996; Schotsmans, 1999). It is in this moment that the Self can recognise its own good in the good of the Other and become truly human through recognition of the Other.

In this illustration, clear connections emerge between the Self's attempt to impose itself on the Other and the imposition of the religious, medical and social models of disability on the lives of disabled people. When the temporarily abled encounter and recognise the difference of the disabled Other, rather than attempting to impose their own ways of being onto the unknown, both the Self and the Other gain access to a myriad of possibilities (Baldwin and Estey–Burtt, 2013, forthcoming). For example, one need only engage with Bob Flanagan's performance art to be faced with a challenge to social (and perhaps one's own) reaction to difference and the unknown. Flanagan's extreme masochism, expressed in painful violence and sado–masochistic sexuality (see for example Dick, 1997, or Flanagan, 2000), challenges heteronormativity and may be discomfiting even for those who may espouse a libertarian perspective. In his poem *Why? A poem by Bob Flanagan*, Flanagan gives a series of possible answers to the question 'Why do you do it?' These answers, always partial and contingent, sometimes contradictory or conflictual, serve to draw attention to Flanagan's creation of Self by disrupting standard narratives of what it means to be disabled and point to a myriad of possibilities. (For a lengthy exposition on Bob Flanagan, see McRuer, 2006, an altogether more comfortable read than Flanagan's own work.)

For Deleuze and Guattari (1987), this multiplicity is expressed in the term 'lines of flight' – a number of possibilities that human beings have the opportunity to construct and reconstruct 'in accordance with desire and in response to their circumstances'. Rather than being constrained by the limited type of being of the meta-narratives described earlier, disabled people are free to build and shape their own narratives that need be neither linear nor limited:

> To me, in my life reality, thinking about my disability as a rhizomatic formation is useful and productive.... Without knowing what specific assemblages will emerge for any one reader-operator, a rhizomatic model allows the co-existence of "not only different regimes of signs but also states of things of differing status" (Deleuze and Guattari, Plateaus, 7) – and that last part of the quote, things of different status, resonates with my lived experience of disability as one that lives in a simultaneity of codes, devalued and valued at the same time. The rhizomatic model of disability produces an abundance of meanings that do not juxtapose pain and pleasure or pride and shame, but allow for an immanent transformation, a coming into being of a state of life in this world, one that is constantly shifting and productive of new subject/individual positions.... It is a movement rather than a definition. (Kuppers, 2009, p 226)

In this we come to the crip theory of McRuer (2006, p 31) which resists 'delimiting the kinds of bodies and abilities that are acceptable or that will bring about change', expressed in the lives of Sharon Kowalski challenging normalised forms of family, Gary Fisher repudiating the notion and desirability of rehabilitation and, of course, Bob Flanagan, supermasochist.

Further reflections

The three meta-narratives discussed in this chapter will be familiar, as models, to many readers. By reframing these models in the language of narrative we have attempted to pave the way for a counterstory, based on Deleuzo-Guattarian rhizomatics (see Chapter 3). This counterstory, however, is not singular and is not attempting to provide an alternative meta-narrative, but to carve out space in which individuals can author their own stories within a supportive narrative environment or web of locution. Rhizomatics allows for the creative assembly of elements from all aspects of life, without trying to frame these within a pre-determined model of what counts as an acceptable narrative. This is, we believe, more in line with the social work values such as empowerment, social justice and liberation. Such an approach does not mean, however, that anything goes. While service users should be encouraged and supported to create their own lives free from limiting meta-narratives, it would be contradictory to allow such creations to become oppressive stories for others. In working with service users to free themselves, social workers also need to work with service users to understand the limits of those freedoms and, ideally, to join with others to work toward mutual freedoms.

If, as social workers and people interested in social work practice, we claim to be interested in the promotion of 'social change, problem solving in human relationships and the empowerment and liberation of people to enhance well-being' (BASW, 2002, p 1), then establishing a perspective on disability that ensures the respect for the personhood of all individuals is of utmost importance. Since narrative, by virtue of its flexibility, allows the rhizomatic nature of human beings discussed earlier to be taken into account, we suggest that narrative is an integral tool for understanding the lives of disabled people.

Note

[1] While the literature talks about models of disability we wish to substitute the term meta-narrative for a number of reasons. The notion of models suggests that each model is discrete, relatively fixed, objective and applicable. The notion of meta-narratives as summaries of social and cultural shared understandings allows for room within each narrative for fissures, contradictions, nuances and so on within which alternatives can arise. The notion of meta-narrative allows also for a dynamism that is lost in the notion of models – narratives interact, morph, recuperate oppositional narratives, open up certain spaces and close down others through strategic choices and the deployment of rhetoric (see Plummer, 1994). So, while the language in this chapter at times might appear strange, we ask the reader to remember that we are not simply attempting to substitute one word for another, or force the discourse surrounding disability into a narrative framework where it does not belong, but are attempting to capture something different to the notion of models.

Conclusion

Narrative, as I indicated at the beginning of the book, is ubiquitous. Not only do narratives give us information about ourselves, others and the world, but narrative as a perspective and process also shapes what we experience and enables us to imbue the world with meaning. This view of narrative is relatively uncontroversial. The strong programme – that narrative *constitutes* the Self and the world – being the stance I have taken in this book is, perhaps, more contentious, but I hope to have demonstrated how this programme helps makes sense of social work by exploring how narrative is inextricably linked with social work values of human rights and social justice, how it shapes who we are and how we relate to others, how ethical reasoning can emerge from understanding individual stories and the narrative webs or narrative environment in which they are located, and how narrative features in areas of social work such as child protection, mental health and disability. In bringing this book to a close I look, very briefly, at some of the advantages and dangers of that programme.

With regard to the advantages of a narrative perspective I hope that I have managed to indicate these as I have gone along, but a summary here will not go amiss. First, narrative seems well suited as a means of understanding social work. A number of writers have commented on the essentially narrative nature of social work (for example, Hall, 1997; Wilks, 2005; and more indirectly, Pithouse, 1987; Pithouse and Atkinson, 1988), but most of these, Hall (1997) being the exception, have not dug deep to uncover the narrative roots from which social work springs. In Chapter 2 I demonstrated how narrative aligns well with the values and principles of social work as they are laid out in the BASW *Code of ethics*, especially in the links between human rights and voice. Similarly, narrative also converges with social work's commitment to social justice in that narrative operates on many levels at once, and can explain structural, discoursal and macro-sources of discrimination and oppression, understand the impact of these on the individual and create spaces in which to construct counter-narratives, empowering, and expressing solidarity with, service users. Examples of this are given in Chapter 2 but also in Chapter 7 in relation to narrative, social work and mental health. Narrative, in its flexibility and closeness to experience, can accommodate and embrace diversity in ways that other frameworks cannot. In Chapter 4, for example, we saw how the uniqueness of the ethical encounter between the Self and Other is incorporated into the ethical reasoning process based on the dual concepts of the Said and the Saying. In this way, individual, community and cultural diversity is inherently respected.

A second key advantage is that narrative is essentially agentic, that is, it allows, and creates space, for individuals and groups to be active in the construction of their own narrative. A narrative approach is possible even with those whose ability to articulate verbally has been compromised (see Chapter 2 on the narrative dispossession of people living with dementia). To be sure, narratives can, and do, oppress individuals, but this is not a function of narratives per se but the outworkings of power that determine what constitutes a recognisable narrative and which narratives can be heard and how. By drawing on Plummer's sociology of stories we can begin to explore these processes and their impact on the process and product of narrative. There is nothing inherent within narrative that requires the silencing of other narratives, other voices. Narrative, in this way, is a great equaliser – given the opportunity and a level of narrative literacy on the part of the reader/listener, almost everyone can participate.

Third, narrative can encapsulate complexity, nuance, paradox, multiplicity and irony. Whether on the level of an individual story of difficult circumstances or in searching for explanations of how organisations work (or not) or how professional and other discourses operate via narrative does not require the simplification or reduction of events, ideas and phenomena to templated forms. Again, this may well happen, as we saw in Chapter 6, but also again, there is nothing inherent in a narrative perspective that requires this to happen. Indeed, one might argue that such simplification and reduction is contrary to the human right to a narrative voice (Chapter 2). Social work is a complex activity and, as I hope to have demonstrated, narrative can help us understand that complexity.

Further, narrative is reflexive in that all narratives have a narrative – we can tell stories about storytelling. Indeed, we see such reflexivity in articles about the 'narrative turn' (see, for example, Hyvärinen, 2006, 2010). In this way it is possible to apply the same forms of analysis to narrative analysis as narrative analysis applies to other data. So, for example, one could analyse my text here in terms of plot, characterisation, rhetoric and so on. This reflexivity, I believe, helps authors maintain a symmetry of approach between competing stories. In the case of P, C & S discussed in Chapter 6, the social workers and judge approached the competing narratives of the mother and the paediatrician a–symmetrically – that is, from the outset they privileged the 'expert' narrative over the lay narrative. In laying this charge, it would be inappropriate for me to ask the reader to privilege my narrative in a similar manner. Reflexivity and the possibility of competing narratives contributes to the quality of narratives being written – if an author seeks to persuade the reader, then the work must strive to be of a higher quality than the competition, evaluated symmetrically.

As much as I am committed to narrative as an approach to scholarly activity, however, I am very aware that there are significant unresolved issues in the literature. I have skated over these in the body of this book as its purpose was not to write a text about narrative per se but to demonstrate how narrative can be applied to social work. However, before concluding, I think it a matter of probity to at least point the reader in the direction of some of the criticisms of, and dangers within, a narrative approach in the hope that readers will be enthused enough to want to read and understand more about narrative and its relevance.

First of all, while many authors seem to subscribe to Barthes' view of the ubiquity of narrative (see the Introduction), there are some that view narrative as having a more limited extent. In the literature about the Self, for instance,

Strawson (2004) argues against the notion of the narrative Self, at least as being universally applicable, presenting the case that some people see their lives as episodic rather than narrative in nature. Zahavi (2007) argues that there are notions of the Self that cannot be captured in narrative fashion, and Dershowitz (1996) argues that life is not a dramatic narrative but consists of much that is inconsequential, meaningless and un-narratable. In defence of the narrative Self I think it important to note that Strawson's conception of the narrative Self is that of the essentialist Self discussed in Chapter 3, a Self that is stable, linear and cohesive. This, we have seen, has its problems, but this does not result in having to abandon a concept of the narrative Self, as I have tried to argue in the section on the rhizomatic Self (Chapter 3) . Indeed, Strawson's episodic Self can be seen as being constituted from smaller narratives that are more transient than those involved in the essentialist Self. Similarly, while we can agree with Dershowitz that much of life is not a dramatic narrative, this does not mean that life is not narratively constituted. Life may not be dramatic for much of the time, and in this Dershowitz may have a point, but even the mundane can be narrativised. For Zahavi there is some part of experience that is pre-narrative, but even assuming one accepts it, there is the question of how one is to access that experience, if not through narrative (see Crites, 1971).

Taking ethics as a second example, there are those who accept that narrative has a place but who do not see narrative as a distinct ethical framework in its own right. In this view narrative can aid ethical decision-making but cannot provide the normative framework that ethics requires (see, for example, Arras, 1997; Childress, 1997). There have been attempts to establish criteria by which competing narratives can be ethically evaluated (see Hauerwas, 1977) but these, to date, have remained somewhat vague, and much work is needed both theoretically and empirically to develop narrative ethics.

On a more general level, even if we take a more limited view of narrative there is still the question as to whether narrative reflects or constitutes the world. In other words, is the world as postmodern as narrative seems to imply? Or are there stories that can be told that are better (not simply more persuasive) because they better reflect reality? Is it a matter, simply, of preferred realities, as Freedman and Combs (1996) suggest, or are there objective factors that we need to take into account when forming our narratives? This is important for social workers who are called to promote social justice, for if feminist, structuralist and Marxist critiques are simply meta-narratives competing for acceptance rather than reflecting material or ideational oppressions, then there is little basis on which to choose one over the other, or how to synthesise approaches. If all is rhetoric, then how do we make rational choices? These questions will, I guess, never be satisfactorily answered. There have been attempts at times to argue why some positions are better than others – for example, Harris' (1979) defence of Marxism, drawing on the philosophy of Imre Lakatos, where Harris claims Marxism meets Lakatos' criteria for a generative research programme and is thus superior to other paradigms that do not – but on the whole these fundamental philosophical arguments do not find their way into mainstream social work literature.

Linked to this sense of relativism is the problem that narrative does not, and perhaps cannot, provide guidelines for action. If, for example, the encounter between two narrative Selves is so unique, à la Levinas (see Chapter 4), then how can a profession provide norms and standards to protect both service users and practitioners? Is it reasonable to expect that social workers take on the sole and infinite responsibility for their practice, as Levinas' argument would have us do? To be sure, such an approach would prevent re-occurrences of poor practice being defended as established organisational procedure (for an extreme example of this, see Gurney, 2012), but practitioners would also be laid open to impropriety without any benchmark against which to make such an evaluation. The question thus becomes, if we want to persist in, and insist on, a narrative approach, how can we establish narrative criteria on which to evaluate practice and conduct?

It is also important to acknowledge the seductive nature of narrative. We have seen (Chapter 6) how a coherent narrative focusing on a clear central action can be more persuasive than a more fragmentary narrative, even though that coherence was bought at the price of glossing over complexity and smoothing of detail. When narrative invokes not only claims to factuality but also draws on the rhetoric of ethos and pathos, it is sometimes difficult to disentangle on what grounds we are persuaded to adopt or accept the narrative. Being 'seduced by narrative' is a danger not only in the courtroom (see Kadoch, 2000) but also in day-to-day practice where service users might seek to manipulate the social worker or excuse or explain their behaviour, inviting the social worker to collude with them in their exculpatory narrative. Such seduction, of course, also operates between professionals where articulate narratives, sharing similar values as our own, might be believed regardless of their evidentiary or explanatory merit (see Chapter 6).

Having said all that I invite you, the reader, to re-read the text, applying the analysis laid out in preceding chapters to what I have discussed. In Chapter 1 I suggested that narrative carries its own form of rhetoric in its structure, its language, its content, its level of detail, its use of ethos and pathos as persuasive techniques and so on. Throughout this text I have used narrative techniques such as comparison and irony to present my argument. In Chapter 6, for example, I constructed an alternative narrative to explain the events of P, C & S – an exercise in emplotment – presented the mother far differently than she was presented in the actual proceedings (ethos) – and have, at least implicitly, appealed to a sense of injustice (pathos). Whether the narrative I have presented here is more or less persuasive than that of the original hearings is yet to be decided, but I think it only fair that my arguments, my narratives, be subject to the same form of analysis that I have here applied to others.

Similarly, how has the structure of the book acted rhetorically? I have deliberately chosen to move from social work values, that is, the very nature of social work, through the environment in which social work occurs (ethics and policy) before applying narrative theory to areas of social work activity. Has this process had a cumulative effect that has made the latter chapters more persuasive than they might otherwise have been? Of course, I do not have any answers to these questions as these answers lie with the reader's interpretation of the text – all I can do is raise the question in the hope of generating the same sort of critique of this text as I have undertaken of others.

Further, have the examples on which I have drawn been ones that resonate with your experience, or with stories you have previously heard and accepted? Certainly there will be stories that make more sense, are more acceptable because they are familiar and/or canonical. Others will be less familiar and possibly outside of current experience. I would invite you to ask yourself how familiarity or strangeness of the narratives I have presented here has influenced your reception of my argument.

These are only some of the narrative features of this book and only some of the narrative techniques I have quite deliberately used in order to make my argument. Again, is my argument stronger because of these? Again, that is for you to determine. I have told a story about the importance of narrative in social work – my role as author is now done. As readers yours is not. Adapting what Thomas King (2003, p 29) says about each of the stories, he tells:

> The story is now yours. Do with it what you will. Tell it to friends. Turn it into a television movie. Forget it. But don't say in the years to come that you would have done things differently if only you had heard this story. You've heard it now.

References

Abbott, H.P. (2002) *The Cambridge introduction to narrative*, Cambridge: Cambridge University Press.

Abels, P. and Abels, S.L. (2001) *Understanding narrative therapy: A guidebook for the social worker*, New York: Springer.

Allen, W. (1983) *Zelig*, Los Angeles, CA: Orion Pictures Corporation.

Allison, D. and Roberts, M. (1998) *Disordered mother or disordered diagnosis? Munchausen by proxy syndrome*, Hillsdale, NJ: Analytic Press.

Alzheimer's Australia Vic (2008) *Perceptions of dementia in ethnic communities*, Hawthorn, Victoria: Alzheimer's Australia Vic (www.fightdementia.org.au/common/files/NAT/20101201-Nat-CALD-Perceptions-of-dementia-in-ethnic-communities-Oct08.pdf).

Alzheimer's Society (2008) *Dementia: Out of the shadows*, London: Alzheimer's Society.

Aristotle (nd) 'Rhetoric', Reproduced in R. McKeon (ed) (2001) *The basic works of Aristotle*, New York: The Modern Library.

Arnett, R. and Arneson, P. (1999) *Dialogic civility in a cynical age: Community, hope, and interpersonal relationships*, Albany, NY: SUNY Press.

Arras, J. (1997) 'Nice story, but so what? Narrative and justification in ethics', in H.L. Nelson (ed) *Stories and their limits: Narrative approaches to bioethics*, New York: Routledge, pp 65-88.

Atkinson, P. (1995) *Medical talk and medical work*, London: Sage Publications.

Bailey, R. and Brake, M. (1975) *Radical social work*, New York: Pantheon Books.

Bainbridge, L. (1999) 'Competing paradigms in mental health education and practice', in B. Pease and J. Fook (eds) *Transforming social work practice: Postmodern critical perspectives*, London: Routledge, pp 179-94.

Bakhtin, M.M. (1986) *Speech genres and other late essays* (translated by V.W. McGee), Austin, TX: University of Texas Press.

Baldwin, C. (1996) 'Munchausen syndrome by proxy: Problems of definition, diagnosis and treatment', *Health and Social Care in the Community*, vol 4, no 3, pp 159-65.

Baldwin, C. (2000) 'Munchausen syndrome by proxy: Telling tales of illness', Unpublished PhD thesis, Sheffield: Department of Sociological Studies, University of Sheffield.

Baldwin, C. (2004) 'Narrative analysis and contested allegations of Munchausen syndrome by proxy', in B. Hurwitz, T. Greenhalgh and V. Skultans (eds) *Narrative research in health and illness*, Oxford: Blackwell Publishing, pp 205-22.

Baldwin, C. (2005) 'Who needs fact when you've got narrative? The case of P, C & S vs United Kingdom', *International Journal for the Semiotics of the Law*, vol 18, nos 3-4, pp 217-41.

Baldwin, C. (2006a) 'Professional insincerity, identity and the limits of narrative repair', in R. Robinson, N. Kelly and K. Milnes (eds) *Narrative and memory*, Huddersfield: University of Huddersfield, pp 13-22.

Baldwin, C. (2006b) 'The narrative dispossession of people with dementia: Thinking about the theory and method of narrative', in K. Milnes, C. Horrocks, N. Kelly, B. Roberts and D. Robinson (eds) *Narrative, memory and knowledge: Representations, aesthetics and contexts*, Huddersfield: University of Huddersfield, pp 101-9.

Baldwin, C. (2008a) 'Rhetoric, child protection and the violation of human rights', *British Journal of Community Justice*, vol 6, no 1, pp 35-48.

Baldwin, C. (2008b) 'Narrative(,) citizenship and dementia: The personal and the political', *Journal of Aging Studies*, vol 22, no 3, pp 222-8.

Baldwin, C. (2011) 'Narrative rhetoric in expert reports: A case study', *Narrative Works*, vol 1, no 2, pp 3-20.

Baldwin, C. and Estey-Burtt, B. (2013: forthcoming) 'The ethics of caring' in A. Thomas and T. Dening (eds) *The Oxford textbook of old age psychiatry* (5th edn), Oxford: Oxford University Press.

Bamberg, M. (2004) 'Talk, small stories, and adolescent identities', *Human Development*, vol 47, no 6, pp 366-9.

Banks, S. (1998) 'Professional ethics in social work – what future?', *British Journal of Social Work*, vol 28, no 2, pp 213-31.

Banks, S. (2006) *Ethics and values in social work* (3rd edn), Basingstoke: Palgrave Macmillan.

Barrett, R. (1996) *The psychiatric team and the social definition of schizophrenia: An anthropological study of person and illness*, Cambridge: Cambridge University Press.

Barthes, R. (1977) 'Introduction to the structural analysis of narratives', in R. Barthes (ed) *Image-Music-Text*, London: Fontana Press.

Bartlett, E.J. and Wilson, J.C. (1982) *A study of narrative rhetoric: Final report* (www.eric.ed.gov/PDFS/ED234414.pdf).

Bartlett, R. and O'Connor, D. (2007) 'From personhood to citizenship: Broadening the lens for dementia practice and research', *Journal of Aging Studies*, vol 21, no 2, pp 107-18.

Baruch, G. (1981) 'Moral tales: parents' stories of encounters with the health professions', *Sociology of Health & Illness*, vol 3, no 3, pp 275-95.

BASW (British Association of Social Workers) (2002) *Code of ethics* (http://cdn.basw.co.uk/membership/coe.pdf).

BASW (2011) *The ethics of social work: Principles and standards* (www.basw.co.uk/codeofethics/).

Beauchamp, T.L. and Childress, J.F. (2001) *Principles of biomedical ethics* (5th edn), Oxford: Oxford University Press.

Beckham, M. (1981) *Tiny revolutions*, Manchester: Granada Television.

Belkin, L. (2010), 'Should Down Syndrome be cured?', Motherlode: Adventures in Parenting, *The New York Times* (http://parenting.blogs.nytimes.com/2010/01/11/should-down-syndrome-be-cured).

Benford, R.D. (2002) 'Controlling narratives and narratives as control within social movements', in J.E. Davis (ed) *Stories of change: Narrative and social movements*, Albany, NY: SUNY Press, pp 53-75.

Bennett, W.L. and Feldman, M.S. (1981) *Reconstructing reality in the courtroom: Justice and judgment in American culture*, New Brunswick, NJ: Rutgers University Press.

Benso, S. (1996) 'Of things face-to-face with Levinas face-to-face with Heidegger: Prolegomena to a metaphysical ethics of things', *Philosophy Today*, vol 40, no 1, pp 132-41.

Berger, L. (2011) 'The lady, or the tiger? A field guide to metaphor and narrative', *Washburn Law Journal*, vol 50, no 2, pp 275-318.

Beresford, P. and Croft, S. (1980) *Community control of social services departments*, London: Battersea Community Action.

Bergeron, M.L. (1996) 'Hegemony, lay and psychiatry: A perspective on the systematic oppression of "rogue mothers"', in S. Aaron (ed) *Feminist Legal Studies*, vol IV, no 1, pp 49-72.

Berkenkotter, C. and Ravotas, D. (1997) 'Genre as tool in the transmission of practice over time and across professional boundaries', *Mind, Culture, and Activity*, vol 4, no 4, pp 256-74.

Bex, F.J. (2009) 'Analyzing stories using schemes', in H. Kaptein, H. Prakken and B. Verheij (eds) *Legal evidence and proof: Statistics, stories, logic*, Aldershot: Ashgate Publishing Limited, pp 93-116.

Blakemore-Brown, L. (1997) 'Munchausen syndrome by proxy', *The Psychologist*, vol 10, no 9, p 391.

Blakemore-Brown, L. (1998) 'False illness in children – or simply false accusations?', *The Therapist*, vol 5, no 2, pp 24-9.

Bohlmeijer, E., Westerhof, G.J., Randall, W., Tromp, T. and Kenyon, G. (2011) 'Narrative foreclosure in later life: Preliminary considerations for a new sensitizing concept', *Journal of Aging Studies*, vol 25, no 4, pp 364-70.

Bond, J. (1992) 'The medicalization of dementia', *Journal of Aging Studies*, vol 6, no 4, pp 397-403.

Booth, T. and Booth, W. (1996) 'Sounds of silence: Narrative research with inarticulate subjects', *Disability & Society*, vol 11, no 1, pp 55-69.

Booth, W. (1961) *The rhetoric of fiction*, Chicago, IL: University of Chicago Press.

Boseley, S. (2009) 'Dementia strategy criticised by Alzheimer's trust', *The Guardian*, 3 February (www.guardian.co.uk/lifeandstyle/2009/feb/03/dementia-alzheimers-antipsychotic).

Bourdieu, P. (1986) 'The forms of capital', in J.G. Richardson (ed) *Handbook for theory and research for the sociology of education*, New York: Greenwood, pp 241-58.

Bourdieu, P. and Passeron, J.C. (1990) *Reproduction in education, society and culture*, London: Sage Publications.

Brake, M. and Bailey, R. (1975) *Radical social work*, New York: Pantheon Books.

Brandon, D. (1991) *Innovation without change? Consumer power in psychiatric services*, Basingstoke: Palgrave Macmillan.

Braverman, H. (1974) *Labour and monopoly capital: The degradation of work in the twentieth century*, New York: Monthly Review Press.

Breunlin, R., Himelstein, A. and Nelson, A. (2008) '"Our stories, told by us": The neighbourhood story project in New Orleans', in R. Solinger, M. Fox and K. Irani (eds) *Telling stories to change the world: Global voices on the power of narrative to build community and make social justice claims*, New York: Routledge, pp 75-89.

Bridgman, T. and Barry, D. (2002) 'Regulation is evil: An application of narrative policy analysis', *Policy Sciences*, vol 35, no 2, pp 141-61.

Brock, D. (1993) *Life and death: Philosophical essays in biomedical ethics*, Cambridge: Cambridge University Press.

Brooker, D. (2005) 'Dementia care mapping: A review of the research literature', *The Gerontologist*, vol 45, suppl 1, pp 11-18.

Bruner, J. (1987a) 'Life as narrative', *Social Research*, vol 54, no 1, pp 11-32.

Bruner, J. (1987b) *Actual minds, possible worlds*, Cambridge, MA: Harvard University Press.

Bruner, J. (1990) *Acts of meaning: Four lectures on mind and culture*, Cambridge, MA: Harvard University Press.

Bruner, J. (2006) 'A narrative model of self-construction', *Annals of the New York Academy of Sciences*, vol 818, no 1, pp 145-61.

Burke, R.D. (1995) *When the music's over: My journey into schizophrenia*, New York: HarperCollins Publishers.

Burton, T. (2003) *Big fish*, Los Angeles, CA: Columbia Pictures Corporation.

Bury, M. (1982) 'Chronic illness as biographical disruption', *Sociology of Health & Illness*, vol 4, no 2, pp 167-82.

Butler, J. (1989) *Gender trouble: Feminism and the subversion of identity*, New York: Routledge.

Cabinet Office (2008) *Excellence and fairness: Achieving world class public services*, Norwich: The Stationery Office.

Calvino, I. (1981) *If on a winter's night a traveler*, New York: Harcourt Brace Jovanovich.

Camp, C.J. (2006) 'Spaced retrieval: A case study in dissemination of a cognitive intervention for persons with dementia', in D. Koltai Attix and K.A. Welsch-Bohmner (eds) *Geriatric neuropsychological assessment and intervention*, New York, NY: The Guilford Press, pp 275-92.

Campling, P. (2001) 'Therapeutic communities', *Advances in Psychiatric Treatment*, vol, no 5, pp 365-72.

Cannan, C. (1975) 'Welfare rights and wrongs', in R. Bailey and M. Brake (eds) *Radical social work*, New York: Pantheon Books, pp 112-28.

Cantor, C. and Baume, P. (1999) 'Suicide prevention: A public health approach', *Australian and New Zealand Journal of Mental Health Nursing*, vol 8, no 2, pp 45-50.

Cast, A.D. (2003) 'Power and the ability to define the situation', *Social Psychology Quarterly*, vol 66, no 3, pp 185-201.

Charon, R. (1994) 'Narrative contributions to medical ethics: recognition, formulation, interpretation, and validation in the practice of the ethicist', in E.R. DuBose, R. Hamel and L.J. O'Connell (eds) *A matter of principles? Ferment in US bioethics*, Valley Forge, PA: Trinity Press International, pp 260-83.

Charon, R., Trautman Banks, J., Hunsaker Hawkins, A., Montgomery Hunter, K., Hudson Jones, A., Montello, M. and Poirer, S. (1995) 'Literature and medicine: Contributions to clinical practice', *Annals of Internal Medicine*, vol 122, no 8, pp 599-606.

Chatman, S. (1978) *Story and discourse: Narrative structure in fiction and film*, London: Cornell University Press.

Cheston, R. and Bender, M. (1999) *Understanding dementia: The man with the worried eyes*, London: Jessica Kingsley Publishers.

Cheston, R., Jones, K. and Gilliard, J. (2003) 'Group psychotherapy and people with dementia', *Aging and Mental Health*, vol 7, no 6, pp 452-61.

Childress, J.F. (1997) 'Narrative(s) versus norm(s): A misplaced debate in bioethics', in H.L. Nelson (ed) *Stories and their limits: Narrative approaches to bioethics*, New York: Routledge, pp 252-71.

Clapton, J. and Fitzgerald, J. (2012) 'The history of disability: A history of "otherness"', *New Renaissance Magazine* (www.ru.org/human-rights/the-history-of-disability-a-history-of-otherness.html).

Clark, L.W. (1995) 'Interventions for persons with Alzheimer's disease: Strategies for maintaining and enhancing communicative process', *Topics in Language Disorders*, vol 15, no 2, pp 47-65.

Clay, G.R. (2000) 'In defense of flat characters: A discussion of their value to Charles Dickens, Jane Austen, and Leo Tolstoy', *International Fiction Review*, vol 27, no 1-2.

Clouser, K.D. and Gert, B. (1990) 'A critique of principlism', *Journal of Medicine and Philosophy*, vol 25, no 2, pp 219-36.

Cohen, B. (2008) *Mental health, user narratives: New perspectives on illness and recovery*, Basingstoke: Palgrave Macmillan.

Conrad, P. (2007) *The medicalization of society*, Baltimore, MD: The Johns Hopkins University Press.

Cooper, C., Selwood, A., Blanchard, M., Walker, Z., Blizard, G. and Livingston, G. (2009) 'Abuse of people with dementia by family carers: Representative cross sectional survey', *British Medical Journal*, vol 339, no 7694, pp 1-5.

Coppock, V. and Hopton, J. (2000) *Critical perspectives on mental health*, London: Routledge.

Corrigan, P. and Leonard, P. (1978) *Social work practice under capitalism: A Marxist approach*, Basingstoke: Macmillan.

Covey, H.C. (2005) 'Western Christianity's two historical treatments of people with disabilities or mental illness', *Social Science Journal*, vol 42, no 1, pp 107-14.

Cresswell, J. and Baerveldt, C. (2011) 'Bakhtin's realism and embodiment: Towards a revision of the dialogical self', *Culture & Psychology*, vol 17, no 2, pp 263-77.

Crites, S. (1971) 'The narrative quality of experience', *Journal of the American Academy of Religion*, vol 39, no 3, pp 291–311.

Czarniawska, B. (1999) *Writing management: Organization theory as a literary genre*, Oxford: Oxford University Press.

Czarniawska, B. (2004) *Narrative in social science research*, London: Sage Publications.

DasGupta, S. and Charon, R. (2004) 'Personal illness narratives: Using reflective writing to teach empathy', *Academic Medicine*, vol 79, no 4, pp 351-6.

Davis, C. (1996) *Levinas: An introduction*, Cambridge: Polity Press.

Davis, J.E. (2002) *Stories of change: Narrative and social movements*, Albany, NY: SUNY Press.

Davis, L. (2006) 'Introduction: The need for disability studies', in L. Davis (ed) *The disability studies reader* (2nd edn), New York: Routledge, pp xv–xviii.

de Souza Ramos, J., de Faria Pereira Neto, A. and Bagrichevsky, M. (2011) 'Pro-anorexia cultural identity: The characteristics of a lifestyle in a virtual community' (translated by M. Aparecida Gazotti Vallim), *Interface – Comunicação, Saúde, Educação, Botucatu*, vol 15, no 37, pp 447-60.

de Witt Spurgin, S. (1993) *The power to persuade: A rhetoric and reader for argumentative writing* (3rd edn), Upper Saddle River, NJ: Prentice Hall.

Deleuze, G. and Guattari, F. (1987) *A thousand plateaus: Capitalism and schizophrenia* (translated by B. Massumi), Minneapolis, MN: University of Minnesota Press.

Delgado, R. (1989) 'Storytelling for oppositionists and others: A plea for narrative', *Michigan Law Review*, vol 87, no 8, pp 2411-41.

Dementia UK (2011) *Life story work* (www.dementiauk.org/information-support/life-story-work/).

Dershowitz, A.M. (1996) 'Life is not a dramatic narrative', in P. Brooks and P. Gerwitz (eds) *Law's stories: Narrative and rhetoric in the law*, New Haven, CT: Yale University Press, pp 99-105.

DH (Department of Health) (2008) *Carers at the heart of 21st-century families and communities*, London: DH Publications.

DH (2009a) *Living well with dementia: A National Dementia Strategy*, London: DH Publications.

DH (2009b) *Consultation response and analysis: National Dementia Strategy*, London: DH Publications.

Dick, K. (1997) *SICK: The life and death of Bob Flanagan, supermasochist*, Santa Monica, CA: Lionsgate Films.

Diedrich, W.W., Burggraeve, R. and Gastmans, C. (2006) 'Towards a Levinasian care ethic: A dialogue between the thoughts of Joan Tronto and Emmanuel Levinas', *Ethical Perspectives*, vol 13, no 1, pp 33-61.

Donham, S. (2009) 'A "cure" for Down syndrome?', *Contrarian* (http://contrarian.ca/2009/11/27/a-cure-for-down-syndrome-%E2%80%94-reader-feedback-4/).

Downs, M., Small, N. and Froggatt, K. (2006) 'Person–centred care for people with severe dementia', in A. Burns and B. Winblad (eds) *Severe dementia*, London: Wiley & Sons, pp 193-204.

Dunford, R. and Jones, D. (2000) 'Narrative in strategic change', *Human Relations*, vol 53, no 9, pp 1207-26.

Ellis, C., Adams, T.E. and Bochner, A.P. (2011) 'Autoethnography: An overview', Forum: *Qualitative Social Research*, vol 12, no 1 (www.qualitative-research.net/index.php/fqs/article/view/1589/3095).

Engel, J.D., Zarconi, J., Pethtel, L.L. and Missimi, S.A. (2008) *Narrative in health care: Healing patients, practitioners, profession, and community*, Oxford: Radcliffe Publishing.

England, H. (1986) *Social work as art: Making sense for good practice*, London: Allen & Unwin.

Evans, J.H. (2000) 'A sociological account of the growth of principlism', *The Hastings Center Report*, vol 30, no 5, pp 31-8.

Ewick, P. (1995) 'Subversive stories and hegemonic tales: Toward a sociology of narrative', *Law and Society Review*, vol 29, no 2, pp 197-226.

Ewick, P. and Silbey, S. (2003) 'Narrating social structure: Stories of resistance to legal authority', *American Journal of Sociology*, vol 108, no 6, pp 1328-72.

Fine, G.A. (2002) 'The storied group: Social movements as "bundles of narratives"', in J.E. Davis (ed) *Stories of change: Narrative and social movements*, Albany, NY: SUNY Press, pp 229-45.

Fischer, F. (2003) *Reframing public policy: Discursive politics and deliberative practices*, New York: Oxford University Press.

Fisher, G. and Mitchell, I. (1995) 'Is Munchausen syndrome by proxy really a syndrome?', *Archives of Disease in Childhood*, vol 72, no 6, pp 530-4.

Fisher, W.R. (1984) 'Narration as a human communication paradigm: The case of public moral argument', *Communication Monographs*, vol 51, no 1, pp 1-22.

Fisher, W.R. (1985) 'The narrative paradigm: An elaboration', *Communication Monographs*, vol 52, no 4, pp 347-67.

Flanagan, B. (2000) *Bob Flanagan: Supermasochist*, New York: Juno Press.

Forster, E.M. (1927) *Aspects of the novel*, New York: Harcourt, Brace & Company.

Foucault, M. (1977) *Discipline and punish*, New York: Vintage.

France, C.M. and Uhlin, B.D. (2006) 'Narrative as an outcome domain in psychosis', *Psychology and Psychotherapy*, vol 79, no 1, pp 53-67.

Frank, A. (1995) *The wounded storyteller: Body, illness, and ethics*, Chicago, IL: University of Chicago Press.

Freedman, J. and Combs, G. (1996) *Narrative therapy: The social construction of preferred realities*, New York: W.W. Norton & Company.

Freeman, M. (2000) 'When the story's over: Narrative foreclosure and the possibility of self-renewal', in M. Andrews, S. Slater, C. Squire and A. Treacher (eds) *Lines of narrative: Psychosocial perspectives*, London: Routledge, pp 81-91.

Freeman, M. (2010) *Hindsight: The promise and peril of looking back*, New York: Oxford University Press.

Freeman, M. (2011) 'Narrative foreclosure in later life: Possibilities and limits', in G. Kenyon, E. Bohlmeijer and W.L. Randall (eds) *Storying later life: Issues, investigations, and interventions in narrative gerontology*, New York: Oxford University Press, pp 3-19.

Freire, P. (1972) *Pedagogy of the oppressed*, Harmondsworth: Penguin Books.

Freire, P. (1974) *Education for critical consciousness*, London: Sheed and Ward.

Furedi, F. (2006) 'The end of professional dominance', *Society*, vol 43, no 6, pp 14-18.

Galilee, J. (2006) 'Literature review on media representations of social work and social workers', Edinburgh: Scottish Executive.

Garland-Thomson, R. (2002) 'Integrating disability, transforming feminist theory', *NWSA Journal*, vol 14, no 3, pp 1-32.

Geertz, C. (1974) 'From the native's point of view: On the nature of anthropological understanding', *Bulletin of the American Academy of Arts and Sciences*, vol 28, no 1, pp 26-45.

Genette, G. (1972) *Figures III*, Paris: Seuils.

Gibson, W. and Smith, M. (2005) *Stelarc: The monograph*, Cambridge, MA: The MIT Press.

Gillon, R. (1994) 'Medical ethics: Four principles plus attention to scope', *British Medical Journal*, vol 309, no 6948, pp 184-7.

Goffman, E. (1963) *Stigma: Notes on the management of spoiled identity*, Englewood Cliffs, NJ: Prentice-Hall, Inc.

Goffman, E. (1974) *Frame analysis: An essay on the organization of experience*, Cambridge, MA: Harvard University Press.

Goggin, G. and Newell, C. (2004) 'Uniting the nation? Disability, stem cells, and the Australian media', *Disability & Society*, vol 19, no 1, pp 47-60.

Good, P. (2001) *Language for those who have nothing: Mikhail Bakhtin and the landscape of psychiatry*, New York: Springer.

Goodley, D. (1996) 'Tales of hidden lives: A critical examination of life history research with people who have learning difficulties', *Disability & Society*, vol 11, no 3, pp 333-48.

Goodley, D. (2007a) 'Becoming rhizomatic parents: Deleuze, Guattari and disabled babies', *Disability & Society*, vol 22, no 2, pp 145-60.

Goodley, D. (2007b) 'Towards socially just pedagogies: Deleuzoguattarian critical disability studies', *International Journal of Inclusive Education*, vol 11, no 3, pp 317-34.

Goodley, D. (2010) *Disability studies: An interdisciplinary introduction,* London: Sage Publications Ltd.

Gordon, D. and Parreno, P. (2006) *Zidane*, Paris: Anna Lena Films.

Gorman, J. (1993) 'Postmodernism and the conduct of inquiry in social work', *Affilia*, vol 8, no 3, pp 247-64.

Gregory, M. (2009) *Shaped by stories: The ethical power of narratives*, Notre Dame, IN: University of Notre Dame Press.

GSCC (General Social Care Council) (2010) *Specialist standards and requirements for post-qualifying social work education and training: Social work in mental health services*, London: GSCC.

Gullette, M. (2004) *Aged by culture*, Chicago, IL: University of Chicago Press.

Gurney, M. (2012) 'Police arrest and stripsearch innocent man after child doodles a gun', *National Post*, 24 February (http://fullcomment.nationalpost. com/2012/02/24/matt-gurney-police-arrest-and-stripsearch-innocent-man-after-child-doodles-a-gun/).

Hall, C. (1997) *Social work as narrative: Storytelling and persuasion in professional texts*, Aldershot: Ashgate.

Hall, C., Sarangi, S. and Slembrouck, S. (1997) 'Moral construction in social work discourse', in B.L. Gunnarsson, P. Linell and B. Nordberg (eds) *The construction of professional discourse,* London: Addison Wesley Longman Ltd, pp 265-91.

Hall, C., Slembrouck, S. and Sarangi, S. (2006) *Language practices in social work: Categorisation and accountability in child welfare*, London: Routledge.

Haller, B. (1995) 'Rethinking models of media representations of disability', *Disability Studies Quarterly*, vol 15, no 2, pp 26-30.

Hampton, G. (2011) 'Narrative policy analysis and the use of the meta-narrative in participatory policy development within higher education', *Higher Education Policy*, vol 24, no 3, pp 347-58.

Hardy, T. (2008) *Tess of the D'Urbervilles*, Oxford: Oxford University Press.

Harman, G. (2009) *Prince of networks: Bruno Latour and metaphysics*, Melbourne: re.press.

Harris, J. (1985) *The value of life: An introduction to medical ethics*, London: Routledge.

Harris, J. (2003) 'In praise of unprincipled ethics', *Journal of Medical Ethics*, vol 29 no 5, pp 303-6.

Harris, K. (1979) *Education and knowledge*, London: Routledge.

Hashmi, M. (2009) 'Dementia: an anthropological perspective', *International Journal of Geriatric Psychiatry*, vol 24, no 2, pp 207-12.

Hassan, T. (2008) 'An ethic of care critique', *Quest Proceedings*, SUNY (http:// dspace.sunyconnect.suny.edu/bitstream/handle/1951/43954/An_Ethic_of_ Care_Critique.pdf?sequence=1).

Hauerwas, S. (1977) *Truthfulness and tragedy: Further investigations into Christian ethics*, Notre Dame, IN: University of Notre Dame Press.

Haynes, F. and McKenna, T. (eds) (2001) *Unseen genders: Beyond the binaries*, New York: Peter Lang Publishing.

Herman, D. (2002) *Story logic: Problems and possibilities of narrative*, Lincoln, NE: University of Nebraska Press.

Hermans, H.J.M. (2002) 'The dialogical self as a society of the mind', *Theory and Psychology*, vol 12, no 2, pp 147-60.

Hermans, H.J.M., Kempen, H.J.G. and van Loon, R.J.P (1992) 'The dialogical self: Beyond individualism and rationalism', *American Psychologist*, vol 47, no 1, pp 23-33.

Heydt, M. and Sherman, N.E. (2005) 'Conscious use of self: Tuning the instrument of social work practice with cultural competence', *The Journal of Baccalaureate Social Work*, vol 10, no 2, pp 25-40.

Hines, S. (2006) 'What's the difference? Bringing particularity to queer studies of transgender', *Journal of Gender Studies*, vol 15, no 1, pp 49-66.

Holma, J. and Aaltonen, J. (1995) 'The self-narrative and acute psychosis', *Contemporary Family Therapy*, vol 17, no 3, pp 307-16.

Hunter, K.M. (1991) *Doctors' stories: The narrative structure of medical knowledge*, Princeton, NJ: Princeton University Press.

Hyden, L.C. (1997) 'The institutional narrative as drama', in B.L. Gunnarsson, P. Linell and B. Norberg (eds) *The construction of professional discourse*, Harlow: Addison Wesley Longman Limited, pp 245-64.

Hyden, L.C. (2010) 'Identity, self, narrative', in M. Hyvarinen, L. Hyden, M. Saarenheimo and M. Tamboukou (eds) *Beyond narrative coherence*, Amsterdam: John Benjamins, pp 33-48.

Hyvärinen, M. (2006) 'Towards a conceptual history of narrative'. Collegium: Studies across Disciplines in the Humanities and Social Sciences, vol 1 (https://helda.helsinki.fi/bitstream/handle/10138/25742/001_04_hyvarinen. pdf?sequence=1).

Hyvärinen, M. (2010) 'Revisiting narrative turns', *Life Writing*, vol 7, no 4, pp 69-82.

Hyvärinen, M., Hyden, L., Saarenheimo, M. and Tamboukou, M. (2010) 'Beyond narrative coherence: An introduction', in M. Hyvärinen, L. Hyden, M. Saarenheimo and M. Tamboukou (eds) *Beyond narrative coherence*, Amsterdam: John Benjamins, pp 1-15.

IFSW (International Federation of Social Workers) (2004) *Statement of ethical principles* (http://ifsw.org/policies/code-of-ethics/).

Ignatieff, M. (1996) 'Articles of faith', *Index on Censorship*, vol 25, no. 5, pp 110-22.

Ikels, C. (2002) 'Constructing and deconstructing the self: Dementia in China', *Journal of Cross-Cultural Gerontology*, vol 17, no 3, pp 233-51.

Illich, I. (1975) *Tools for conviviality*, London: Fontana/Collins.

Illich, I. (1976) *Deschooling society*, Harmondsworth: Penguin.

Illich, I. (1977) *Limits to medicine: Medical nemesis – The expropriation of health*, Harmondsworth: Penguin.

Illich, I. (1996) *In the vineyard of the text: A commentary of Hugh's Didascalion*, Chicago, IL: University of Chicago Press.

Illich, I., Zola, I.K., McKnight, J., Caplan, J. and Shaiken, H. (1977) *Disabling professions*, London: Marion Boyars.

Ineichen, B. (1996) 'The prevalence of dementia and cognitive impairment in China', *International Journal of Geriatric Psychiatry*, vol 11, no 8, pp 695-7.

Ingleby, D. (1985) 'Professionals as socializers: The "psy complex"', in S. Spitzer and A.T. Scull (eds) *Research in law, deviance and social control*, vol 7, London: JAI Press, pp 79-109.

James, H. (1884) 'The art of fiction', *Longman's Magazine*, no 4 (September) [reprinted in *Partial portraits* (1888)] (http://virgil.org/dswo/courses/novel/james-fiction.pdf).

Jarvik, L.F. and Winograd, C.H. (eds) (1988) *Treatment for the Alzheimer patient: The long haul*, New York: Springer Publishing Company.

Kadoch, L.C. (2000) 'Seduced by narrative: Persuasion in the courtroom', *Drake Law Review*, vol 49, no 1, pp 71-123.

Kaplan, T.J. (1993) 'Reading policy narratives: Beginnings, middles and ends', in F. Fischer and J. Forester (eds) *The argumentative turn in policy analysis and planning*, London: UCL Press, pp 167–85.

Keady, J. and Williams, S. (2005) 'Co-constructed inquiry: A new approach to the generation of shared knowledge in chronic illness', Paper presented at RCN International Research Conference, Belfast, 8–11 March.

Ketokivi, K. (2008) 'Biographical disruption, the wounded self, and the reconfiguration of significant others', in E. Widmer and K. Jallinoja (eds) *Beyond the nuclear family: Families in a configurational perspective*, Bern: Peter Lang AG, pp 255–78.

King, T. (2003) *The truth about stories: A native narrative*, Toronto, ON: House of Anansi Press.

Kitwood, T. (1990) 'Understanding senile dementia: A psychobiographical approach', *Free Associations*, 19, pp 60–76.

Kitwood, T. (1996) 'A dialectical framework for dementia', in R.T. Woods (ed) *Handbook of clinical psychology of ageing*, London: John Wiley & Sons, pp 267–82.

Kitwood, T. (1997) *Dementia reconsidered: The person comes first*, Maidenhead: Open University Press.

Kuppers, P. (2009) 'Toward a rhizomatic model of disability: Poetry, performance, and touch', *Journal of Literary and Cultural Disability Studies*, vol 3, no 3, pp 221–40.

La Fontaine, J.S. (1998) *Speak of the devil: Tales of satanic abuse in contemporary England*, Cambridge: Cambridge University Press.

Landon, B. (2008) *Building great sentences: Exploring the writer's craft*, Chantilly, VA: Teaching Company.

Langan, M. and Lee, P. (1989) *Radical social work today*, London: Unwin Hyman.

Latour, B., Harman, G. and Erdélyi, P. (2011) *The prince and the wolf: Latour and Harman at the LSE*, London: Zero Press.

Leach, M. and Mearns, R. (eds) (1996) *The lie of the land: Challenging received wisdom on the African environment*, Oxford: James Currey.

Leitch, V., Cain, W., Finke, L., Johnson, B., McGowan, J. and Williams, J. (2001) *The Norton anthology of theory and criticism*, New York: W.W. Norton & Company, Inc.

Leonard, P. (1984) *Personality and ideology*, London: Macmillan.

Levinas, E. (1961) *Totality and infinity*, Pittsburgh, PA: Dusquesne University Press.

Lewis, B. (2011) *Narrative psychiatry: How stories can shape clinical practice*, Baltimore, MD: The Johns Hopkins University Press.

Little, J.N. and Hoskins, M.L. (2004) '"It's an acceptable identity": Constructing "girl" at the intersections of health, media, and meaning-making', *Child and Youth Services*, vol 26, no 2, pp 75–93.

Locke, J. (1836/1964) *An essay concerning human understanding*, London: Oxford University Press.

Lockyer, F. (nd) 'Why the conviction?' (www.sallyclark.org.uk/why.html).

Lukes, S. (1974) *Power: A radical view*, Basingstoke: Macmillan.

Lyman, K.A. (1989) 'Bringing the social back in: A critique of the biomedicalization of dementia', *The Gerontologist*, vol 29, no 5, pp 597–605.

Lyotard, J.-F. (1984) *The postmodern condition: A report on knowledge* (translated by G. Bennington and B. Massumi), Manchester: Manchester University Press.

Lysaker, P., Wicket, A., Wilke, N. and Lysaker, J. (2003) 'Narrative incoherence in schizophrenia: The absent agent–protagonist and the collapse of internal dialogue', *American Journal of Psychotherapy*, vol 57, no 2, pp 153-66.

Lyttle, J. (1986) *Mental disorder: Its care and treatment*, London: Baillière Tindall.

MacIntyre, A. (1984) *After virtue: A study in moral theory*, Notre Dame, IN: University of Notre Dame Press.

McAdams, D.P. (2006) 'The redemptive self: Generativity and the stories Americans live by', *Research in Human Development*, vol 3, no 2-3, pp 81-100.

McDonough, J.E. (2001) 'Using and misusing anecdote in policy making', *Health Affairs*, vol 20, no 1, pp 207-12.

McGranahan, C. (2010) 'Narrative dispossession: Tibet and the gendered logics of historical possibility', *Comparative Studies in Society and History*, vol 52, no 4, pp 768-97.

McKnight, J. (1995) *The careless society: Community and its counterfeits*, New York: Basic Books.

McRuer, R. (2006) *Crip theory: Cultural signs of queerness and disability*, New York: New York University Press.

Mandell, D. (2007) *Revisiting the use of self: Questioning professional identities*, Toronto: Canadian Scholars' Press Inc.

Markula, P. (2006) 'The dancing body without organs: Deleuze, femininity, and performing research', *Qualitative Inquiry*, vol 12, no 1, pp 3-27.

Mart, E. (2002) *Munchausen's syndrome by proxy reconsidered*, Manchester, NH: Bally Vaughan Publishing.

Martin, J., Feldman, M., Hatch, M.J. and Sitkin, S.B. (1983) 'The uniqueness paradox in organizational stories', *Administrative Science Quarterly*, vol 28, no 4, pp 418-53.

Meadow, R. (1977) 'Munchausen syndrome by proxy: The hinterland of child abuse', *Lancet*, vol 2, 13 August, pp 343-5.

Metzler, I. (2006) *Disability in Medieval Europe: Thinking about physical impairment during the high Middle Ages, c. 1100-1400*, Abingdon: Routledge.

Miehls, D. and Moffatt, K. (2000) 'Constructing social work identity based on the reflexive self', *British Journal of Social Work*, vol 30, no 3, pp 339-48.

Mills, M.A. (1998) *Narrative identity and dementia. A study of autobiographical memories and emotions*, Aldershot: Ashgate Publishing.

Montello, M. (1997) 'Narrative competence', in H.L. Nelson (ed) *Stories and their limits: Narrative approaches to bioethics*, London, Routledge, pp 185-97.

Moore, A. (1989) 'Trial by schema: Cognitive filters in the courtroom', *UCLA Law Review*, vol 37, no 273, pp 273-341.

Moore, L.A. and Davis, B. (2002) 'Quilting narrative: Using repetition techniques to help elderly communicators', *Geriatric Nursing*, vol 23 no 5, pp 262-6.

Morley, C.J. (1995) 'Practical concerns about the diagnosis of Munchausen syndrome by proxy', *Archives of Disease in Childhood*, vol 72, no 6, pp 528-9.

Morley, C.J. and Macfarlane, S. (2010) 'Repositioning social work in mental health: Challenges and opportunities for critical practice', *Critical Social Work*, vol 11, no 2, pp 46-59.

Morris, C. (1972) *The discovery of the individual 1050-1200*, Toronto: University of Toronto Press.

Mullaly, R.P. (2007) *The new structural social work*, Don Mills, ON: Oxford University Press.

Mullan, F. (1999) 'Me and the system: The personal essay and health policy', *Health Affairs*, vol 18, no 4, pp 118-24.

Mumby, D. (1987) 'The political function of narrative in organizations', *Communication Monographs*, vol 9, no 2, pp 113-27.

Murphy, J., Tester, S., Hubbard, G., Downs, M. and MacDonald, C. (2005) 'Enabling frail older people with a communication difficulty to express their views: The use of Talking Mats™ as an interview tool', *Health and Social Care in the Community*, vol 13, no 2, pp 95-107.

Nelson, H.L. (2001) *Damaged identities, narrative repair*, Ithaca, NY: Cornell University Press.

Nelson, H.L. (2002) 'Context: Backwards, sideways, and forward', in R. Charon and M. Montello (eds) *Stories matter: The role of narrative in medical ethics*, New York: Routledge, pp 39-47.

Newton, A.Z. (1995) *Narrative ethics*, Cambridge, MA: Harvard University Press.

Noddings, N. (1995) *Caring: A feminine approach to ethics and moral education*, Berkeley, CA: University of California Press.

Norberg, A., Melin, E. and Asplund, K. (2003) 'Reactions to music, touch and object presentation in the final stage of dementia: An exploratory study', *International Journal of Nursing Studies*, vol 40, no 5, pp 473-9.

Northern Officer Group Report (2002) *Disability studies*, University of Leeds (www.leeds.ac.uk/disability-studies/archiveuk/Northern%20Officers%20 Group/defining%20impairment%20and%20disability.pdf).

O'Reilly, E. (1997) *Sobering tales*, Amherst, MA: University of Massachusetts Press.

Oaks, D. (2011) 'The moral imperative for dialogue with organizations of survivors of coerced psychiatric human rights violations', in T.W. Kallert, J.E. Mezzich and J. Monahan (eds) *Coercive treatment in psychiatry: Clinical, legal and ethical aspects*, Chichester: John Wiley & Sons, Ltd.

Oliver, M. (1983) *Social work with disabled people*, Basingstoke: Macmillan.

Paré, A. (1998) 'Discourse regulations and the production of knowledge', in R. Spika (ed) *Writing in the workplace: New research perspective,* Carbondale, IL: Southern Illinois University Press, pp 111-22.

Paré, A. (2000) 'Writing as a way into social work', in P. Dias and A. Paré (eds) *Transitions: Writing in academic and workplace settings,* Cresskill, NJ: Hampton Press, pp 145-66.

Parker, J. and Bradley, G. (2010) *Social work practice: Assessment, planning, intervention and review*, Exeter: Learning Matters.

Parker, S., Pease, B. and Fook, J. (1999) 'Empowerment: The modernist social work concept *par excellence*', in B. Pease and J. Fook (eds) *Transforming social work practice: Postmodern critical perspectives*, London: Routledge, pp 150-7.

Parrott, L. (2010) *Values and ethics in social work practice* (2nd edn), Exeter: Learning Matters.

Parsons, T. (1951) *The social system*, Glencoe, IL: The Free Press.

Parton, N. and O'Byrne, P. (2000) *Constructive social work: Towards a new practice*, Basingstoke: Macmillan.

Passarinho, I. (2008) 'Social worker – paths and identity construction', *Sísifo: Educational Sciences Journal*, vol 6, pp 21-34.

Phelan, R. (2006) 'Narrative theory, 1966-2006: A narrative', in R. Scholes and R. Kellogg, *The nature of narrative* (40th anniversary edn), New York: Oxford University Press, pp 283-336.

Pidd, H. (2012) 'Jersey child abuse victims to receive compensation', *The Guardian*, 29 March (www.guardian.co.uk/uk/2012/mar/29/jersey-child-abuse-victims-compensation).

Pirandello, L. (1921/1998) *Six characters in search of an author*, New York: Dover Publications, Inc.

Pithouse, A. (1987) *Social work: The social organisation of an invisible trade*, Aldershot: Avebury.

Pithouse, A. and Atkinson, P. (1988) 'Telling the case: Occupational narrative in a social-work office', in N. Coupland (ed) *Styles of discourse*, London: Croom Helm, pp 183-200.

Plummer, K. (1994) *Telling sexual stories: Power, change, and social worlds*, London: Routledge.

Poindexter, C.C. (2002) 'Meaning form methods: Re-presenting narratives of an HIV-affected caregiver', *Qualitative Social Work*, vol 1, no 1, pp 59-78.

Poliandri, S. (2011) *First Nations, identity, and reserve life: The Mi'kmaq of Nova Scotia*, Lincoln, NE: University of Nebraska Press.

Polkinghorne, D.E. (1988) *Narrative knowing and the human sciences*, Albany, NY: SUNY Press.

Polkinghorne, D.E. (1995) 'Narrative configuration in qualitative analysis', in J.A. Hatch and R. Wisniewski (eds) *Life history and narrative*, London: Falmer Press, pp 5-24.

Polletta, F. (2002) 'Plotting protest: Mobilizing stories in the 1960 student sit-ins', in J.E. Davis (ed) *Stories of change: Narrative and social movements*, Albany, NY: SUNY Press, pp 31-51.

Post, F. (1983) 'The clinical assessment of mental disorders', in M. Shepherd and O.L. Zangwill (eds) *Handbook of psychiatry, Vol 1, General psychopathology*, pp 210-20, Cambridge: Cambridge University Press.

Post, S.G. (2000) *The moral challenge of Alzheimer disease: Ethical issues from diagnosis to dying* (2nd edn), Baltimore, MD: The Johns Hopkins University Press.

Powell, J.L. and Edwards, M.M. (2002) 'Policy narratives of aging: The right way, the third way or the wrong way?', *Electronic Journal of Sociology*, vol 6 (www.sociology.org/content/vol006.001/powell-edwards.html).

Power, J. (2009) 'A "cure" for Down syndrome?', *Contrarian* (http://contrarian.ca/2009/11/27/a-cure-for-down-syndrome-%E2%80%94-reader-feedback-6/).

Propp, V. (1968) *Morphology of the folktale* (translated by L. Scott), Austin, TX: University of Texas Press.

Pyrhönen, H. (2007) 'Genre', in D. Herman (ed) *The Cambridge companion to narrative*, Cambridge: Cambridge University Press, pp 109-23.

Ramsay, R. (2003) 'Transforming the working definition of social work into the 21st century', *Research on Social Work Practice*, vol 13, no 3, pp 324-38.

Redford, A. (1976) *Labour migration in England, 1800-1850*, Manchester: Manchester University Press.

Rennell, T. (2008) 'Brothers at war: The WW1 soldier and the pacifist ... but who was the hero?', *Mail Online*, 14 February (www.dailymail.co.uk/news/article-514300/Brothers-war-The-WW1-soldier-pacifist--hero.html).

Reupert, A. (2007) 'Social worker's use of self', *Clinical Social Work Journal*, vol 35, no 2, pp 107-16.

Richardson, M. and Beresford, P. (1978) *Deschooling social work*, London: Battersea Community Action.

Ricoeur, P. (1976) *Interpretation theory: Discourse and the surplus of meanings*, Fort Worth, TX: Texas Christian University Press.

Ricoeur, P. (1985) *Time and narrative, Vol 2* (translated by K. McLaughlin and D. Pellaver), Chicago, IL and London: University of Chicago Press.

Ricoeur, P. (1991) 'Life in quest of narrative', in D. Wood (ed) *On Paul Ricoeur: Narrative and interpretation*, London: Routledge, pp 29-33.

Riessman, C.K. and Quinney, L. (2005) 'Narrative in social work: A critical review', *Qualitative Social Work*, vol 4, no 4, pp 391-412.

Robbins, B.D. (2000) *Emmanuel Levinas* (http://mythosandlogos.com/Levinas.html).

Roberts, G.A. (2000) 'Narrative and severe mental illness: What place do stories have in an evidence-based world?', *Advances in Psychiatric Treatment*, vol 6, no 6, pp 432-41.

Roberts, M. (2006) 'Gilles Deleuze: Psychiatry, subjectivity, and the passive synthesis of time', *Nursing Philosophy*, vol 7, no 4, pp 191-204.

Robson, C. (2002) *Real world research: A resource for social scientists and practitioner-researchers* (2nd edn), Oxford: Blackwell.

Roe, E. (1988) 'Deconstructing budgets', *Diacritics*, vol 18 no 2, pp 61-8.

Roe, E. (1991) 'Development narratives, or making the best of blueprint development', *World Development*, vol 19, no 4, pp 287-300.

Roe, E. (1994) *Narrative policy analysis, theory and practice*, Durham, NC and London: Duke University Press.

Roscoe, K.D. (2009) *Critical social work practice: A narrative approach*, Wrexham: Glyndwr University Research Online (http://epubs.glyndwr.ac.uk/cgi/viewcontent.cgi?article=1016&context=chcr).

Roscoe, K.D., Carson, A.M. and Madoc-Jones, L. (2011) 'Narrative social work: Conversations between theory and practice', *Journal of Social Work Practice: Psychotherapeutic Approaches in Health, Welfare and the Community*, vol 25, no 1, pp 47-61.

Rose, H. (1973) 'Up against the welfare state: The claimant unions', *The Socialist Register*, vol 10, pp 179-203.

Rosseel, E. (2001) *Het onschatbare subject. Aspecten van het postmoderne zelf* [*The invaluable subject. Aspects of the postmodern self*], Brussels, Belgium: VUBpress.

Ryan, E.B., Bannister, K.A. and Anas, A.P. (2009) 'The dementia narrative: Writing to reclaim social identity', *Journal of Aging Studies*, vol 23, no 3, pp 145-57.

Ryan, M.A. (2004) 'Beyond a Western bioethics?', *Theological Studies*, vol 65, no 1, pp 158-77.

Ryan, T.M. (1997) 'Munchausen syndrome by proxy: Misogyny or modern medicine?', *The Association of Trial Lawyers of America's Women Trial Lawyers Caucus Newsletter*, Fall, nos 3-4.

S.H. (nd) *Whose body is it anyway?* (http://ampulove.net/information/dev-wan-whos-body.htm).

Salgado, J. and Clegg, J. (2011) 'Dialogism and the psyche: Bakhtin and contemporary psychology', *Culture & Psychology*, vol 17, no 4, pp 421-40.

Sandelowski, M. (1994) 'We are the stories we tell. Narrative knowing in nursing practice', *Journal of Holistic Nursing*, vol 12, no 1, pp 23-33.

Schechtman, M. (1996) *The constitution of selves*, Ithaca, NY: Cornell University Press.

Schneider, D.C. (2009) *Quantitative ecology: Measurement, models, and scaling* (2nd edn), Boston, MA: Academic Press.

Scholes, R. and Kellogg, R. (2006) *The nature of narrative* (40th anniversary edn), New York: Oxford University Press.

Schotsmans, P. (1999) 'Personalism in medical ethics', *Ethical Perspectives*, vol 6, no 1, pp 10-20.

Schreier, H. and Libow, J. (1993) *Hurting for love: Munchausen by proxy syndrome*, New York: Guilford Press.

Schwabenland, C. (2006) *Stories, visions and values in voluntary organisations*, Abingdon: Ashgate Publishing Group.

Schweitzer, P. and Bruce, E. (2008) *Remembering yesterday, caring today: Reminiscence in dementia care: A guide to good practice*, London: Jessica Kingsley Publishers.

Sermijn, J., Devlieger, P. and Loots, G. (2008) 'The narrative construction of the self: Selfhood as a rhizomatic story', *Qualitative Inquiry*, vol 14, no 4, pp 632-50.

Shaffer, M.A. and Barrows, A. (2009) *The Guernsey literary and potato peel pie society*, New York: Random House.

Shah, S. and Argent, H. (2006) *Life story work – What it is and what it means*, London: BAAF.

Shakespeare, T. (2006a) *Disability rights and wrongs*, London: Routledge.

Shakespeare, T. (2006b) 'The social model of disability', in L.J. Davis (ed) *The disability studies reader* (2nd edn), New York: Routledge, pp 197-204.

Shakespeare, T. and Watson, N. (2002) 'The social model of disability: An outdated ideology?', *Research in Social Science and Disability*, vol 2, pp 9-28.

Shapiro, J. and Rucker, L.M.D. (2003) 'Can poetry make better doctors? Teaching the humanities and arts to medical students and residents at the University of California, Irvine, College of Medicine', *Academic Medicine*, vol 78, no 10, pp 953-7.

Sharf, B. F. (2001) 'Out of the closet and into the legislature: Breast cancer stories', *Health Affairs*, vol 20, no 1, pp 213-18.

Sherwin, R.K. (1994) 'Law frames: Historical truth and narrative necessity in a criminal case', *Stanford Law Review*, vol 47, no 1, pp 39-83.

Slaughter, J. R. (2007) 'Narration in international human rights law', *CLCWeb: Comparative Literature and Culture*, vol 9, no 1 (http://docs.lib.purdue.edu/clcweb/vol9/iss1/19).

Smith, B. and Sparkes, A. (2008) 'Narrative and its potential contribution to disability studies', *Disability & Society*, vol 23, no 1, pp 17-28.

Soklaridis, S., Cartmill, C. and Cassidy, D. (2011) 'Biographical disruption of injured workers in chronic pain', *Disability and Rehabilitation*, vol 33, nos 23-24, pp 2372-80.

Sokolowski, R. (1989) 'The art and science of medicine', in E. Pellegrino, J. Langan and J. Collins Harvey (eds) *Catholic perspectives on medical morals*, Dordrecht: Kluwer Academic Publishers, pp 263-75.

Solas, J. (1996) 'The limits of empowerment in human service work', *Australian Journal of Social Issues*, vol 31, no 2, pp 147-56.

Solinger, R., Fox, M. and Irani, K. (eds) (2008) *Telling stories to change the world: Global voices on the power of narrative to build community and make social justice claims*, New York: Routledge.

Spence, D.P. (1982) *Narrative truth and historical truth: Meaning and interpretation in psychoanalysis*, New York: W.W. Norton.

Spence, D.P. (1986) 'Narrative smoothing and clinical wisdom', in T. Sarbin (ed) *Narrative psychology: The storied nature of human conduct*, New York: Praeger, pp 211-32.

Stone, B. (2006) 'Diaries, self-talk, and psychosis: Writing as a place to live', *Auto/Biography*, vol 14, no 1, pp 41-58.

Stone, B. (2008) 'Why fiction matters to madness', in G. Robinson, P. Fisher, N. Gilzean, T. Lee, S.J. Robinson and P. Woodcock (eds) *Narratives and fiction: An interdisciplinary approach*, Huddersfield: University of Huddersfield, pp 71-7.

Strawson, G. (2004) 'Against narrativity', *Ration*, vol 17, no 4, pp 428-52.

Strong, P. (1979) *The ceremonial order of the clinic: Parents, doctors, and medical bureaucracies*, London: Routledge & Kegan Paul Books.

Sutton, R. (1999) *The policy process: An overview*, London: Overseas Development Institute (www.eldis.org/vfile/upload/1/document/0708/DOC7279.pdf).

Taylor, C. (1989) *Sources of the self*, Cambridge: Cambridge University Press.

Tekin, S. (2011) 'Self-concept through the diagnostic looking glass: narratives and mental disorder', *Philosophical Psychology*, vol 24, no 3, pp 357-80.

Thornton, T. (2003) 'Psychopathology and two kinds of narrative account of the Self', *Philosophy, Psychiatry, & Psychology*, vol 10, no 4, pp 361-7.

TRC (Truth and Reconciliation Commission) (1998) *Truth and Reconciliation Commission of South Africa report*, vol 1 (www.justice.gov.za/trc/report/finalreport/Volume%201.pdf).

Tremain, S. (2002) 'On the subject of impairment', in M. Corker and T. Shakespeare (eds) *Disability/postmodernity: Embodying disability theory*, London: Continuum International Publishing Group, pp 32-47.

Turner, M. (1991) 'Literature and social work: An exploration of how literature informs social work in a way social sciences cannot', *British Journal of Social Work*, vol 21, no 3, pp 229-43.

Twining, W. (1990) *Rethinking evidence*, Oxford: Blackwell, cited in D.M. Risinger, 'Unsafe verdicts: The need for reformed standards for the trial and review of factual innocence claims', *Harvard Law Review*, vol 41, no 4, pp 1281-336.

UN General Assembly (1948) *Universal Declaration of Human Rights*, 10 December, 217A (III) (www.unhcr.org/refworld/docid/3ae6b3712c.html).

UPIAS (Union of the Physically Impaired Against Segregation) (1975) *Fundamental principles of disability*, London: The Disability Alliance.

Urek, M. (2005) 'Making a case in social work: The construction of an unsuitable mother', *Qualitative Social Work*, vol 4, no 4, pp 451-67.

van Eeten, M.J. (2007) 'Narrative policy analysis', in F. Fischer, G.J. Miller and M.S. Sidney (eds) *Handbook of public policy analysis: Theory, politics, and methods*, Boca Raton, FL: CRC Press, pp 251-88.

van Nijnattan, C. (2007) 'The discourse of empowerment: A dialogical self theoretical perspective on the interface of person and institution in social service settings', *International Journal for Dialogical Science*, vol 2, no 1, pp 337-59.

Walker, T. (2009) 'What principlism misses', *Journal of Medical Ethics*, vol 35, no 4, pp 229-31.

Walton, D. (2006) 'Poisoning the well', *Argumentation*, vol 20, no 3, pp 273-307.

Wasserman, J. (1985) *Caspar Hauser*, New York: Carroll and Graf.

Watson, T. (2002) 'Well, I know this is going to sound very strange to you, but I don't see myself as a disabled person: Identity and disability', *Disability & Society*, vol 17, no 5, pp 509-27.

Wells, K. (2010) 'A narrative analysis of one mother's story of child custody loss and regain', *Children and Youth Services Review*, vol 33, no 3, pp 439-47.

Wells, K. (2011) *Narrative inquiry*, New York: Oxford University Press.

Wells, L.A. (2003) 'Discontinuity in personal narrative: Some perspectives of patients', *Philosophy, Psychiatry, & Psychology*, vol 10, no 4, pp 297-303.

Wheatley, E. (2002) 'Blindness, discipline, and reward: Louis the Ninth and the foundation of the Hospice des Quinze-Vingts', *Disability Studies Quarterly*, vol 22, no 4 (http://dsq-sds.org/article/view/385/518).

Wheatley, E. (2010) *Stumbling blocks before the blind: Medieval constructions of a disability,* Ann Arbor, MI: University of Michigan Press.

White, H. (1973) *Metahistory: The historical imagination in nineteenth-century Europe,* Baltimore, MD: The Johns Hopkins University Press.

White, M. and Epston, D. (1990) *Narrative means to therapeutic ends,* Adelaide: Dulwich Centre Publications.

White, S. (2002) 'Accomplishing the case in paediatrics and child health: Medicine and morality in inter-professional talk', *Sociology of Health & Illness,* vol 24, no 4, pp 409-35.

Whitehouse, P. (2008) *The myth of Alzheimer's: What you aren't being told about today's most dreaded diagnosis,* New York: St Martin's Press.

Wilks, T. (2005) 'Social work and narrative ethics', *British Journal of Social Work,* vol 35, no 8, pp 1249-64.

Williams, S. and Keady, J. (2005) *Co-constructing the early experience of dementia using the CCI approach,* Alzheimer Europe Conference 'Dementia Matters', Kilarney, 9-12 June.

Wyller, T.B. (1997) 'Disability models in geriatrics: Comprehensive rather than competing models should be promoted', *Disability and Rehabilitation,* vol 19, no 11, pp 480-3.

Yan, M.C. and Wong, Y.R. (2005) 'Rethinking self-awareness in cultural competence: Toward a dialogic self in cross-cultural social work', *Families in Society,* vol 86, no 2, pp 181-8.

Zahavi, D. (2007) 'Self and other: The limits of narrative understanding', *Royal Institute of Philosophy Supplement,* vol 82, no 60, pp 179-201.

Index